Evelyn Findlater's
NATURAL FOODS PRIMER

A lively introduction to healthy wholefood eating, with a feast of quick and easy recipes for you to try.

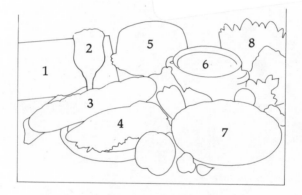

Illustrated on front cover:
1. American Granola (page 12).
2. Apricot, Apple and Yogurt Whip (page 72).
3. Granary French Loaf (page 90).
4. Pitta Breads (page 85).
5. Carob Birthday Cake (page 100).
6. Leek and Potato Soup with Watercress (page 25).
7. Pizza (page 88).
8. Coleslaw (page 65).

Illustrated on back cover: Apple and Apricot Tart (page 81).
Illustrated opposite: Millet Bake (page 36).
Illustrated opposite page 112: Pot Barley and Tomato Broth (page 22).

By the same author
EVELYN FINDLATER'S VEGETARIAN FOOD PROCESSOR

Evelyn Findlater's

NATURAL

FOODS

PRIMER

A Beginner's Guide to Choosing and Using Wholefoods

Illustrated by Paul Kesteven

THORSONS PUBLISHERS LIMITED
Wellingborough, Northamptonshire

First published 1985

British Library Cataloguing in Publication Data

Findlater, Evelyn
　　Evelyn Findlater's natural foods primer.
　　1. Cookery (Natural foods)
　　I. Title
　　641.5'637　　YX741

　　ISBN 0-7225-1162-0

Printed and Bound in Great Britain by
Whitstable Litho Ltd., Whitstable, Kent

CONTENTS

INTRODUCTION

Food is a gift of living. The cooking of it can be a chore because we are so often in a rush to get it over with.

Since the age of sixteen, when I first became responsible for feeding myself, I have enjoyed good food. Not just eating it but choosing and preparing it. I think this love stems from the fact that I was skinny and always hungry when growing up. We had very little fresh fruit and vegetables — in fact, I can still savour the smell and taste of my first banana and orange at the age of six. These were real luxury fruits just after the war. Many of my better fed friends looked at me in amazement at school lunch times because I actually wanted second helpings. But the real interest in a more discerning way of eating came with my first wage packet. On the corner of the office block where I worked there was a stall full of beautiful shiny fruit. As I passed by in the mornings, I saw the fruit being polished and carefully displayed. I bought five shillings worth of these tempting foods and the thrill this gave me is still with me today when I walk through markets which abound with endless varieties of vegetables and fruit.

Although there was little opportunity for me to cook in our family home, and cookery lessons were only once a fortnight and very boring, as soon as I had to cater for myself I began cooking with a passion, read cookery books as some would read exciting novels and fed anyone who would taste my efforts. Of prime importance then was that the end result should taste delicious. I knew nothing about balancing meals, or the need for plenty of fibre in the diet, but through the years I learnt to appreciate what good eating really is and what it does for the body.

To keep the body healthy you need to give it plenty of exercise and feed it with the right food. Enough protein, carbohydrates, an adequate supply of vitamins and minerals are of vital importance to your health. All these you get when you eat natural wholefoods. After all, if you put oil in your petrol tank you will ruin the engine. It is the same with your body. You have to look after it with great care. Using more natural foods in a balanced way will help you do that.

What, then, are these vital natural foods? They are wholefoods, full of nature's own goodness with nothing added to them — such as preservatives, colouring and flavouring — and nothing taken away from them, which happens when food is refined or processed. When you buy white flour you are, in fact, buying a packet of starch, usually with added bleach. The valuable, missing bran, is the fibre which is needed by the body to help get rid of unwanted waste. A lack of this can result in constipation and sometimes lead to more serious illnesses, such as diverticulitis (which is a swelling in the colon wall — most painful) caused by waste matter getting stuck in the intestinal tract. Another important ingredient taken away during processing is wheatgerm, which is jam-packed with vitamins and minerals. And, when you buy white rice, similar important nutrients have been taken from the whole brown rice grain.

In this book I have given nutritional information about particular ingredients used which might be new to a beginner but here is a list of natural wholefoods, and a guide to those rich in fibre.

Fresh fruit and vegetables — rich in fibre.
Dried fruit such as apricots, prunes, figs, dates, sultanas and raisins — rich in fibre.
Dried peas, beans and lentils — rich in fibre.
Nuts and Seeds such as sesame seeds, sunflower seeds — rich in fibre.
Wholegrains such as wholewheat, brown rice, millet and oats — rich in fibre.
Dairy produce, which includes eggs, milk, cheese, butter and yogurt — contains no fibre.
Meat and fish — contain no fibre.

You will note that the last two categories, dairy produce and meat and fish, contain no fibre, so it is important to eat foods rich in fibre if you use these in your recipes and it is equally important to eat plenty of fresh raw vegetables and fruit daily.

Oil, too, plays an important part in your diet. But which are better for your health? There are three categories to remember, saturated, polyunsaturated, and mono-unsaturated fats or oils.

Saturated fats include animal fats, lard, butter, cream and some margarines unless marked 'high in polyunsaturates'. If these are eaten in large amounts they produce a high level of cholesterol in the blood. Now we do need some cholesterol, but if too much is produced then our bodies become more prone to heart attacks and thrombosis. They do not have to be left out of your diet but are best used in moderation.

Polyunsaturated fats: familiar ones include sunflower oil, corn oil, soya oil and vegetable margarines marked 'high in polyunsaturates'. These oils are high in what is called linoleic acid which seems to control the level of cholesterol in the body so use these instead of saturated fats wherever possible.

Olive oil is *mono-unsaturated* and contains mono-unsaturated fatty acids which do not seem to raise the level of cholesterol in our bodies and is easily digested.

Other foods to cut down and avoid as much as possible are sugar and salt. Too much sugar causes tooth decay, obesity and possibly even diabetes. No sugar is good but the darker raw varieties such as Barbados sugar do contain some fibre and small amounts of vitamins and minerals but moderation in using any sugar is vital to your health. Salt is another food to be used sparingly. Too much can raise your blood-pressure which, in turn, can cause heart attacks. Findings have shown that excessive salt consumption can cause arthritis.

The recipes in the book are simple, quick to prepare and, I hope, will be an easy introduction to a healthy way of eating for all beginners, including the young cook in the family. They have been tested by some of my adult cookery students and by children aged ten to fifteen years old, with great success.

Eating wholesome food is as much habit forming as eating chocolate. The more you eat of a particular food the more the body will demand, so it makes sense to give it the chance to crave what is good. This book just touches the surface of healthy eating but I hope it will encourage you to experiment and read about a more natural way of living.

I.

BREAKFAST TIME:
Waking up to a Healthy Start

We have so much to do in a day that it makes sense to give your body a really good energy boost to help it to do what it has to do well. Here are a few recipes to do just that.

Muesli is top of my list at breakfast time. This wonderful cereal is a complete meal in itself and will fill any energy gap throughout the day, not just at breakfast time. The first muesli was made by Dr Bircher-Benner of Zurich in Switzerland, around about the year 1900. He fed his sick patients with a mixture of whole grains, nuts, fresh fruit and milk or yogurt. He firmly believed that a simple, natural diet was the best medicine he could give to help cure those in his care.

The important basic ingredients are whole grains. You can buy what is called *Muesli Base* at any wholefood or healthfood shop. This is simply a mixture of flattened or rolled grains, such as porridge or jumbo oats, toasted wholewheat, barley, rye and millet. This muesli base is then mixed with nuts and seeds, dried chopped fruit, fresh fruit, honey, and natural yogurt or milk. You can try lots of variations, when making your own muesli, to suit your own taste. Make extra if you like it and store the dry ingredients in a jar all ready to add honey, fresh fruit and yogurt or milk just before you serve.

Here are two recipes for making your own muesli, one very simple one and the other a toasted malted cereal, which I think you will love.

Simple Muesli

You will need a mixing bowl, a fork and a thick pan to toast the sunflower seeds and hazel nuts.

Imperial (Metric)	American
2 oz (50g) sunflower seeds	½ cup sunflower seeds
2 oz (50g) chopped hazelnuts	½ cup chopped hazelnuts
8 oz (225g) muesli base	2 cups muesli base
2 oz (50g) raisins or sultanas	⅓ cup dark or golden seedless raisins
2 oz (50g) chopped dates or figs or dried apricots, well washed	⅓ cup chopped dates or figs or dried apricots, well washed
1 rounded tablespoon dark Barbados sugar	1 rounded tablespoon dark Barbados sugar
2 unpeeled eating apples, grated	2 unpeeled eating apples, grated

1 Toast the seeds and nuts in a dry thick pan on a low heat for 10 minutes. Move them around the pan with a wooden spoon.

2 Mix all the dry ingredients together.

3 Finally add the apple and serve with milk or natural (plain) yogurt.

You will not need all the muesli at once. Store any left over dry ingredients in a screw-top jar and add fresh fruit just before serving.

American Granola
(Toasted Malted Muesli)

It's a good idea to make lots of this cereal and store it for several breakfast-times because you will love it. It needs time to toast so make it the day before.

You will need a mixing bowl, one baking tray 8 × 10 inches (20 × 25cm) and one baking tray 12 × 20 inches (30 x 50cm) and one small, thick saucepan.

Imperial (Metric)	American
2 oz (50g) hazelnuts	½ cup hazelnuts
2 oz (50g) sesame seeds	½ cup sesame seeds
2 oz (50g) sunflower seeds	½ cup sunflower seeds
8 oz (225g) porridge oats or muesli base	2 cups rolled oats or muesli base
I oz (25g) wheatgerm	¼ cup wheatgerm
2 oz (50g) bran	½ cup bran
I tablespoon malt extract	I tablespoon malt extract
I tablespoon clear honey	I tablespoon clear honey
2 tablespoons corn or sunflower oil	2 tablespoons corn or sunflower oil
Good pinch of sea salt	Good pinch of sea salt
4 oz (110g) raisins or sultanas	⅔ cup dark or golden seedless raisins

1 Set the oven at 300°F/150°C (Gas Mark 2). Put the nuts and seeds in the small baking tray on the oven shelf just above centre. Toast in the oven until light golden brown — about 30 minutes. Check after 15 minutes and stir to make sure everything is evenly browned.

2 Put the oats, wheatgerm, bran and salt into a mixing bowl.

3 Put the malt, honey and oil in a small thick saucepan. Melt on a low heat until it will pour easily.

4 Trickle the malt liquid over the oat mixture.

5 Stir in well with a fork. Then rub between your fingers until mixture is like rough breadcrumbs.

6 Spread this out on the large baking tray. Your nuts and seeds might be toasted by now. If they are not, put the oat mixture in the oven on the shelf below until the nuts and seeds are ready. Then move the oat mixture to the same shelf on which you toasted your nuts and seeds.

7 Turn the oat mixture with a fork every 15 minutes and leave it toasting for 40 minutes.

8 Mix the oat mixture with the nuts, seeds and raisins or sultanas.

9 Leave to cool and put in a screw-top jar or plastic container with a tight lid. Serve with milk or yogurt.

Sunday Breakfast Pancakes

You will need a small, thick frying pan, a piece of kitchen paper screwed up into a ball and 1 tablespoon corn oil in a dish, ready to oil your pan lightly. Using a pastry brush on hot pans will melt the bristles. You will also need a fish slice, a mixing bowl, a fork and a tablespoon.

Imperial (Metric)	American
2½ oz (65g) porridge oats	⅔ cup rolled oats
2½ oz (65g) wholemeal flour	⅔ cup wholewheat flour
1 completely level tablespoon Barbados sugar	1 completely level tablespoon Barbados sugar
1 rounded teaspoon baking powder	1 rounded teaspoon baking powder
Good pinch of sea salt	Good pinch of sea salt
2 standard eggs, beaten	2 standard eggs, beaten
½ pint (275ml) milk	1⅓ cups milk
2 tablespoons corn or sunflower oil	2 tablespoons corn or sunflower oil

1 Put all the dry ingredients in a bowl.

2 Make a well in the middle and drop in the eggs and one third of the milk.

3 Gradually fold in the dry ingredients towards the liquid in the centre. Mix together thoroughly, adding the rest of the milk and the oil a little at a time.

4 When the batter is smooth, cover and leave to stand for 15 minutes.

5 Stir once more. Your batter is now ready.

6 Grease the pan lightly with the oiled kitchen paper.

7 Heat pan. When hot, turn down heat.

8 Put 2 tablespoons of the pancake batter in the pan tilting it slightly to spread the mixture evenly around the pan. You can use the back of the tablespoon to spread it thinly if you like. Turn up heat at this stage, to cook pancakes quickly.

9 When the top bubbles and the edges curl up and show a tinge of light brown, shake pan. Turn the pancake over with a fish slice. Cook other side for 1 minute only or less.

Note: You can use all wholemeal flour but the oats give a nice texture. It takes practice to make perfect pancakes. It means turning heat up and down as you go along and oiling the pan not too much and not too little. This is very difficult to describe on paper. You will get the knack the more you make.

What to spread on your gorgeous pancakes:
Best served straight from the pan. They will still be good if you stack them on top of each other and keep the lot warm in a low-heated oven. They are great with butter or polyunsaturated margarine, honey and lemon juice, apple juice concentrate, maple syrup, or just soft brown sugar and lemon. Or you could try my Tangy Banana Sauce (page 19) or Apple and Apricot Purée (page 20) spread on your hot pancakes. These are always a winner.

Yogurt

Yogurt has been made and eaten for centuries in Eastern countries such as India and China, in Middle Eastern countries, particularly Syria, Egypt and Lebanon, as well as Bulgaria, Yugoslavia, Greece and Turkey to name just a few. Its true name is *Lactobacillus Bulgaricus* which is quite a mouthful to remember.

Why is yogurt so good for you? Well it produces benevolent bacteria which kills harmful bacteria in our bodies' intestinal tracts. This harmful bacteria can cause illness.

Yogurt also does something else wonderful. It helps to produce Vitamin B in our bodies. You also get Vitamin B from wholemeal bread, whole grains, milk, cheese, eggs, yeast extract, peas, beans and many other foods, so if you are careful with what you eat you will have enough Vitamin B. Unfortunately, Vitamin B is destroyed when we take antibiotics. This can make you feel tired, irritable, have skin rashes and mouth sores. Also, when you are ill you probably do not want to eat many of the foods which have Vitamin B in them, so yogurt is a good stand-by. It's refreshing and very easy to swallow and digest.

To be of any use it must be live natural yogurt, not full of colouring, preservatives or stabilizers, so look at the labels if you are buying yogurt.

Better still, make your own and add fresh fruit or honey for a quick dessert. Here is my recipe to help you make delicious yogurt every time.

Yogurt Making:
A vacuum flask with a wide opening is ideal but not necessary. A glass jar with a wide rim and screw top, or a bowl with a plate to cover will do. You also need a balloon whisk.

Imperial (Metric)	American
1½ pints (850ml) milk	3¾ cups milk
2 tablespoons skimmed milk powder (Makes a thicker yogurt)	2 tablespoons skimmed milk powder (Makes a thicker yogurt)
3 tablespoons fresh live natural yogurt	3 tablespoons fresh live plain yogurt

1 Bring the milk to the boil, then turn down to simmer with the lid off.

2 Simmer for 10 minutes. This helps thicken the yogurt.

3 Cool to a temperature of 110°F (43°C). The milk will still be very warm but should not burn your finger when you test it.

4 Whisk or stir in the milk powder.

5 When it is thoroughly mixed add the yogurt and whisk it well into the milk.

6 Pour this into your chosen container. Make sure that whichever container you use is cleaned with boiling water before you pour in the yogurt mixture.

7 If using a vacuum flask, leave it to stand without moving for 4 to 5 hours. If you are using a glass jar, wrap the jar in a warm, thick towel and stand it upright in a warm place for 4 to 5 hours. (Moving the container will cause the whey to separate and you will have lots of watery yogurt.)

8 When the yogurt is set, put it in the fridge. It will thicken even more as it cools. Again, do not shake it around until it is quite cold.

Porridge
(To warm your toes)

This nourishing hot cereal will give you a warm hearty start on those cold winter mornings.

You will need a thick saucepan and a wooden spoon.

Imperial (Metric)	American
I teacup porridge oats	I cup rolled oats
3 teacups milk	3 cups milk
I heaped tablespoon ground sunflower seeds	I heaped tablespoon ground sunflower seeds
I level tablespoon ground sesame seeds	I level tablespoon ground sesame seeds
I teaspoon sea salt	I teaspoon sea salt
I teaspoon malt extract *or* Barbados sugar	I teaspoon malt extract *or* Barbados sugar

1 Place all ingredients in the saucepan. (If using malt leave that out until the porridge is cooked.)

2 Bring to the boil, on medium heat, stirring all the time.

3 Turn down to low heat and cook gently for 5 minutes. Stir often to stop the porridge sticking.

4 Stir in malt, if using, and mix well. Serve with milk around the edge and a little extra Barbados sugar or honey trickled over the top.

Note: If you have a baby of over six months in the family, just see how they will munch away and still want more.

Now for two tasty fruit sauces to add to your natural yogurt, pancakes or breakfast muesli.

Tangy Banana Sauce

You will need a liquidizer or a mincer for this recipe.

Imperial (Metric)	American
3 oz (75g) sultanas or raisins	½ cup golden or dark seedless raisins
Juice of ½ lemon	Juice of ½ lemon
2 large bananas	2 large bananas
Juice of ½ small orange	Juice of ½ small orange
1 tablespoon apple juice concentrate	1 tablespoon apple juice concentrate
½ teaspoon cinnamon (if you like a spicy taste)	½ teaspoon cinnamon (if you like a spicy taste)

1 Soak the dried fruit in the lemon juice for at least 2 hours.

2 Put all ingredients in the liquidizer and blend on a low speed until you have a smooth sauce. A little honey can be used instead of apple juice concentrate, but use less honey because it is very sweet.

Apple and Apricot Purée

You will need a liquidizer or a mincer for this recipe.

Imperial (Metric)	American
4 oz (110g) dried apricot halves	¾ cup dried apricot halves
½ pint (275ml) boiling water	1¼ cups boiling water
1 tablespoon apple juice concentrate	1 tablespoon apple juice concentrate
2 crisp green eating apples (Golden Delicious are good because the skins are not too tough)	2 crisp green eating apples (Golden Delicious are good because the skins are not too tough)

1 Wash the apricots well in hot running water.

2 Soak the apricots in the water and apple juice concentrate overnight.

3 Drain the apricots and save the juice.

4 Wash the apples, cut and core. Chop into small pieces.

5 Put the apricots, apples and ¼ pint (130ml/⅔ cup) of apricot juice into the liquidizer.

6 Turn to low speed and liquidize to a smooth, thick purée. Add a little more juice if too thick. (If the skins on the apples are very tough then press the purée through a sieve.) The purée will keep in the fridge for 5 days, if it lasts that long without being eaten!

Variation:
Another good idea is to use prunes instead of apricots. Soak in the same way as the apricots, but don't forget to cut the stones out before you liquidize with the apples.

Note: To round off breakfast time if you like a change from tea, coffee or cartons of juice (which cost a lot) turn to page 108 for refreshing herb teas and other drinks.

2.

SOUPS AND SAUCES

Soups

Soups are easy to make so put away that can opener, chop a few vegetables, add a little seasoning, herbs and stock or water and 'hey presto!' you have three batches for the price of one can — and much more nourishing and delicious they are, too.

A liquidizer is a very useful tool to have for soup-making as it brings out that lovely flavour and stops the 'pickers' from flicking out the onions and celery and any other vegetable they don't like. Usually it's not the taste they dislike, but the texture of the vegetables.

There are hundreds of ways of using different ingredients to make delicious soups. I use young nettles, nasturtiums and marigolds and many other wild plants to make very tasty soups, but those recipes are not for this book. Remember that a good cook is prepared to experiment, as I have mentioned before.

Here are four recipes for you to try. If they need liquidizing, then taste them before you purée and again after. You will find such a difference in flavour. It becomes full-bodied and more satisfying. Some soups are much tastier when not puréed but these are for non-pickers. (My first recipe is definitely one of these!)

In the recipes you will see the ingredient stock. This is usually water in which you have boiled other ingredients, but if you do not have this just add a vegetable stock cube to one pint (575ml) of hot water and you will have quick stock ready to use in soups or stews. I also mention shoyu, which is a naturally fermented soya sauce without colouring or flavouring. It adds a delicious flavour to some foods, as you will find out when you try the recipes.

Pot Barley and Tomato Broth

Pot Barley is the whole barley grain. Most people use pearl barley which is refined barley. That is, the bran and most of the germ has been taken away. So try and get pot barley will all its goodness contained in the whole grain. You will need a medium-sized thick saucepan, a wooden spoon and a sharp knife.

Imperial (Metric)	American
2 oz (50g) pot barley	¼ cup pot barley
I pint (575ml) water	2½ cups water
2 tablespoons corn or sunflower oil	2 tablespoons corn or sunflower oil
I medium onion, peeled and finely chopped	I medium onion, peeled and finely chopped
I clove garlic, crushed	I clove garlic, crushed
2 medium carrots, scraped and finely chopped	2 medium carrots, scraped and finely chopped
I medium potato, scrubbed and chopped into ¼ inch (5mm) cubes	I medium potato, scrubbed and chopped into ¼ inch cubes
2 small sticks celery, very finely chopped	2 small stalks celery, very finely chopped
I dessertspoon fresh chopped parsley	2 heaped teaspoons fresh chopped parsley
I teaspoon mixed herbs	I teaspoon mixed herbs
I tin tomatoes (14-oz/400g)	I can tomatoes (14 ounces)
I vegetable stock cube	I vegetable stock cube
½ teaspoon freshly ground black pepper	½ teaspoon freshly ground black pepper
2 teaspoons shoyu (naturally fermented soya sauce)	2 teaspoons shoyu (naturally fermented soy sauce)

1 Soak the barley in the water overnight.

2 Drain off water into a measuring jug and add enough extra water to make it exactly one pint (575ml/2½ cups). Your barley will have absorbed some of the water while it was soaking.

3 Put the oil in a saucepan, heat and add the onion and garlic. Fry gently for 5 minutes with lid on.

4 Add the carrots, potatoes, celery and drained barley. Let this fry gently for 5 minutes.

5 Stir in the parsley and mixed herbs.

6 Chop the tomatoes and stir these into the vegetables. Let the mixture simmer gently with the lid on, while you prepare your stock.

7 Heat your barley water and add the stock cube and black pepper.

8 Add the hot stock to the simmering vegetables. Stir all well together. Simmer for 20 to 25 minutes only.

9 Finally, taste and add the shoyu.

Variations:
This broth is delicious just as it is, but for babies or pickers liquidize some of the soup when it has cooled. At least everyone will be well fed and there will be no grumbles. Serve with Garlic Bread (page 28) and a little cheese for a really tasty and nourishing lunch.

Red Split Lentil Soup

All you will need is a good sized thick saucepan, a wooden spoon, a sharp knife and the liquidizer. If no liquidizer is available then a firm metal sieve will do.

You can use dried green split peas or dried yellow split peas if you do not have red split lentils. Leave out the curry powder if you don't like spicy food, but it's worth a try. Remember you are not just cooking for you.

Imperial (Metric)	American
2 tablespoons corn or sunflower oil	2 tablespoons corn or sunflower oil
1 medium onion, finely chopped	1 medium onion, finely chopped
1 clove of garlic, skinned and chopped very finely	1 clove of garlic, skinned and chopped very finely
2 medium carrots, washed, scraped and very finely chopped	2 medium carrots, washed, scraped and very finely chopped
3 oz (75g) red split lentils, washed well in a sieve	⅓ cup red split lentils washed well in a sieve
1 teaspoon mild curry powder (optional)	1 teaspoon mild curry powder (optional)
1½ pints (850ml) hot vegetable stock	3¾ cups hot vegetable stock
1 tablespoon tomato purée	1 tablespoon tomato paste
1 bay leaf	1 bay leaf
Juice of ½ lemon	Juice of ½ lemon

1 Heat the oil in the saucepan.

2 Add the chopped onion, garlic and carrots. Fry these gently for 5 minutes until soft.

3 Add the lentils, plus the curry powder if you like.

4 Stir all well together with a wooden spoon. Fry for ½ minute. Do not allow to burn.

5 Add the stock, tomatoe purée (paste) and bay leaf.

6 Stir all together. Bring to the boil and quickly turn down to simmer — just bubbling slightly.

7 Put the lid on and cook very gently for about 45 minutes.

8 Finally, add the lemon juice and liquidize the soup when it has cooled.

Note: You do not have to liquidize this soup but it does give it a super flavour.

Leek and Potato Soup with Watercress

You will need a large, thick saucepan, a wooden spoon, a sharp knife and a liquidizer if possible, but a firm metal sieve will do, or just eat it as it is. I love it either way.

Imperial (Metric)	American
2 tablespoons corn or sunflower oil	2 tablespoons corn or sunflower oil
2 medium potatoes, scrubbed and chopped into small pieces	2 medium potatoes, scrubbed and chopped into small pieces
2 small leeks, split, washed and cut in thin rings	2 small leeks, split, washed and cut in thin rings
1 pint (575ml) vegetable stock	2½ cups vegetable stock
½ pint (270ml) milk	1⅓ cups milk
1 bunch watercress (no yellow leaves), washed well	1 bunch watercress (no yellow leaves), washed well
Sea salt and freshly ground black pepper to taste	Sea salt and freshly ground black pepper to taste

1 Heat the oil in the saucepan.

2 Add the potatoes and fry gently for about 5 minutes.

3 Add the leeks and fry for 2 minutes more. Do not allow to burn.

4 Add the hot stock. Bring to boil and quickly turn down to simmer. Cover and cook for 20 minutes.

5 Add the milk and the chopped watercress. (Leave all the stems on the cress, just chop them finely.)

6 Mix all well together, heat through and cook gently with lid off for 2 minutes only. Stir all the time at this stage and do not boil. Taste and season.

7 Let soup cool and serve chilled.

Note: Liquidize if you wish, but taste it before you do. Unliquidized, it will be thin and delicate in flavour. After liquidizing it will be thicker, creamy and strong in flavour. Try it both ways on the family or friends and see what they think.

Sweetcorn Soup or Corn Chowder

This is a sweetish soup which is very popular in America. It is very easy to make and does not need a liquidizer. A balloon whisk to mix the flour and milk is useful.

Imperial (Metric)	American
2 tablespoons corn *or* sunflower oil	2 tablespoons corn *or* sunflower oil
I onion, finely chopped	I onion, finely chopped
2 medium potatoes scrubbed and cut into small pieces	2 medium potatoes scrubbed and cut into small pieces
2 sticks celery with leaves, chopped	2 stalks celery with leaves, chopped
I pint (575ml) vegetable stock	2½ cups vegetable stock
8 oz (225g) frozen sweetcorn	1⅓ cups frozen sweetcorn
I rounded tablespoon wholemeal flour	I rounded tablespoon wholewheat flour
6 fl oz (200ml) milk	¾ cup milk
I level teaspoon dill weed	I level teaspoon dill weed
¼ teaspoon freshly ground nutmeg	¼ teaspoon fresh ground nutmeg
2 heaped tablespoons fresh chopped parsley	2 heaped tablespoons fresh chopped parsley
Sea salt and freshly ground black pepper	Sea salt and freshly ground black pepper

1 Heat the oil in a saucepan. Fry the onions, potatoes and celery gently for 5 minutes.

2 Add the stock and frozen sweetcorn. Bring to the boil, quickly turn down heat and cook gently for 10 minutes with lid on.

3 While this is simmering, whisk the wholemeal flour and the milk in a bowl until there are no lumps.

4 When the soup has simmered for 10 minutes, spoon out 4 tablespoons of the hot liquid and mix it with the milk and flour liquid. Stir well and pour this into the saucepan stirring all the time.

5 Add the dill, nutmeg and parsley. Stir well.

6 Let all cook together gently simmering for 5 more minutes.

7 Finally taste your soup and add a little sea salt and freshly ground black pepper if needed.

Now for some simple recipes which go well with your homemade soups.

Croûtons

You will need a baking tray and a bread knife.

Imperial (Metric)	American
4 slices wholemeal bread	4 slices wholewheat bread
1 oz (25g) polyunsaturated margarine *or* butter	2 tablespoons polyunsaturated margarine *or* butter

1 Set oven at 275°F/140°C (Gas Mark 1).

2 Spread polyunsaturated margarine or butter on the bread slices.

3 Place the slices on top of each other and cut them into ¾ inch (2cm) squares.

4 Spread out pieces on the baking tray.

5 Place in the oven and leave to crisp right through, like babies' rusks. This should take 25 to 35 minutes depending on how fresh the bread is. Arrange your croûtons in a dish and let your guests help themselves.

Simple Garlic Bread

Another tasty accompaniment to soup is Garlic Bread. Now this, of course, is best if you have made your own bread. Turn to page 90 or 85 and see how simple it is to make a Granary French Loaf or Wholemeal and Sesame Seed Bread. But for now I will give you a quick way. Depending on how many you are feeding allow 1 roll per person. My recipes will be enough for four people. You will need a sharp bread knife, a small mixing bowl, some baking foil and a baking tray.

Imperial (Metric)	American
4 wholemeal rolls	4 wholewheat rolls
3 oz (75g) butter *or* polyunsaturated magarine	⅓ cup butter *or* polysunsaturated magarine
3 large cloves garlic, peeled and finely cut and crushed.	3 large cloves garlic, peeled finely cut and crushed.
I dessertspoon fresh parsley, very finely chopped	2 teaspoons freshly parsley, very finely chopped
½ level teaspoon sea salt	½ level teaspoon sea salt
½ level teaspoon freshly ground black pepper (optional)	½ level teaspoon freshly ground black pepper (optional)

1 Set oven 350°F/180°C (Gas Mark 4).

2 Place the margarine or butter in a bowl with the crushed garlic. (To crush garlic, chop finely and then squash the bits with the flat of your knife. Make sure you put the juice *and* pulp into your mixture.)

3 Add parsley, sea salt and freshly ground black pepper.

4 Cream together with a wooden spoon until the mixture is soft and the ingredients smoothed well in together.

5 Cut each roll into six slices, keeping each roll separate from the others.

6 Now butter both sides of each slice.

7 Fit the slices back together to form four rolls again.

8 Wrap each roll, keeping the slices firmly together, in baking foil.

9 Place on baking tray and bake for 10 minutes just before you serve your soup.

Here is a variation on Garlic Bread:

Hot Herb Bread

For this to be really special, my Granary French Loaf (page 90) is necessary, but if you have no time to make it any French loaf will do, preferably wholemeal. Although I have not put garlic in this recipe you can add two cloves, crushed, if you wish. You will need baking foil, a sharp bread knife and a baking tray.

Imperial (Metric)	American
1 medium granary French loaf, or any other French loaf	1 medium granary French loaf, or any other French loaf
3 oz (75g) polyunsaturated margarine or butter	⅓ cup polyunsaturated margarine or butter
½ teaspoon dried basil	½ teaspoon dried basil
½ teaspoon dried tarragon	½ teaspoon dried tarragon
1 dessertspoon fresh chopped parsley	2 teaspoons fresh chopped parsley
1 dessertspoon fresh chopped chives	2 teaspoons fresh chopped chives
½ teaspoon sea salt	½ teaspoon sea salt
½ teaspoon freshly ground black pepper (optional)	½ teaspoon freshly ground black pepper (optional)

1 Set oven to 375°F/190°C (Gas Mark 5).

2 Cut a French loaf at an angle, making the slices ½ inch (1cm) thick. Do not cut each slice right through but leave them joined together by the bottom crust.

3 Cream all the other ingredients to a smooth soft paste. Make sure that everything is well mixed.

4 Carefully spread this herb butter on both sides of your nearly-cut slices.

5 Press the slices gently back into place and put the loaf onto the baking foil and parcel up.

6 Place the wrapped loaf onto a baking tray and bake for 15 to 20 minutes. Serve at once with soup or cheese.

Variations:
Experiment with other herbs such as marjoram, oregano and lemon thyme and you will find your own favourite combination. If you have no fresh chives, you could use the green parts of spring onions (scallions) instead.

Sauces

My first sauce is Tomato Ketchup. I can hear a sigh of relief from those who can't do without it. Well it's very simple to make and will last for two weeks if you keep it in the fridge in a screw-top jar.

Real Tomato Ketchup

Imperial (Metric)	American
12 oz (350g) tomato purée	1⅓ cups tomato paste
4 fl oz (125ml) cider or wine vinegar	½ cup cider or wine vinegar
4 fl oz (125ml) water	½ cup water
1 dessertspoon shoyu	2 teaspoons shoyu
1 teaspoon basil (optional)	1 teaspoon basil (optional)
½ teaspoon ground nutmeg	½ teaspoon ground nutmeg
1 teaspoon mustard powder	1 teaspoon mustard powder
¼ teaspoon freshly ground black pepper	¼ teaspoon freshly ground black pepper
1 clove garlic, very finely crushed or ¼ teaspoon powdered garlic	1 clove garlic, very finely crushed or ¼ teaspoon powdered garlic
1 level teaspoon molasses or dark soft sugar	1 level teaspoon molasses or dark soft sugar
A dash of *Holbrook's* Worcester sauce	A dash of vegetarian Worcester sauce

1 Blend all ingredients together either in a liquidizer or with an egg whisk for 1 minute.

Barbecue Sauce

You will need a big thick saucepan and a liquidizer. This is delicious with any burger or with corn fritters (see page 61 for recipe). It needs quite a few ingredients all of which are important to the final gorgeous taste. Make this for party time or any other special occasion.

Imperial (Metric)	American
I medium onion, peeled and finely chopped	I medium onion, peeled and finely chopped
I clove garlic, peeled and finely chopped	I clove garlic, peeled and finely chopped
2 tablespoon corn oil *or* olive oil	2 tablespoons corn oil *or* olive oil
2 sticks celery, finely chopped	2 stalks celery, finely chopped
½ green pepper, finely chopped	½ green pepper, finely chopped
I teaspoon freshly chopped basil	I teaspoon freshly chopped basil
I heaped tablespoon freshly chopped parsley	I heaped tablespoon freshly chopped parsley
I bay leaf	I bay leaf
I tablespoon lemon juice *or* I tablespoon cider vinegar *or* 2 tablespoons lemon juice	I tablespoon lemon juice *or* I tablespoon cider vinegar *or* 2 tablespoons lemon juice
I tablespoon shoyu	I tablespoon shoyu
I very level dessertspoon molasses	2 teaspoons molasses
14 oz tin tomatoes	14 ounce can tomatoes
2 heaped tablespoons tomato purée	2 heaped tablespoons tomato paste
½ level teaspoon cayenne pepper	½ level teaspoon cayenne pepper
I level teaspoon paprika	I level teaspoon paprika
½ teaspoon mustard powder	½ teaspoon mustard powder
½ teaspoon freshly ground black pepper	½ teaspoon freshly ground black pepper

1 Fry the onion and garlic in the oil, covered, for 5 minutes until soft.

2 Add the celery and fry for 5 more minutes with the lid on.

3 Add the green pepper, basil, parsley and bay leaf and fry for 3 more minutes with lid on.

4 Add all other ingredients, stirring well as you do this.

5 Cover and simmer gently for 30 minutes.

6 Remove the lid, stir well and let simmer for 15 more minutes. This will evaporate some of the liquid and thicken the sauce. Let cool.

7 Remove the bay leaf and purée the sauce in a liquidizer until smooth.

If this doesn't make them lick their lips, nothing will!

3

SAVOURIES FOR LUNCH OR DINNER TIME

This chapter is separated into six parts and will give you a large variety of savoury recipes either for the main meal of the day or a light lunch-time filler.

Whenever possible, try to serve a fresh salad or steamed vegetables with your lunch or main meal dishes. For delicious salads turn to page 63.

Part I — Grains

Another name for grain is cereal. The word cereal comes from Ceres, the Roman goddess of agriculture and the harvest. She was worshipped as the provider of these wonderful plants that grew abundantly and fed so many.

In the Stone Age, man learnt to farm grain crops. This encouraged people to live together in groups rather than travel from place to place as nomadic tribes. The groups lived in small villages and looked after the growing cereals and planted new seeds. Their very early communities were situated around the warm, rich land of the river Nile in Egypt and the Mediterranean countries, because grain grew easily there. Gradually these farming methods spread to other countries, where different varieties of grain grew depending on the climate.

Brown Rice: For thousands of years rice has been a most important food in China and Africa as well as Italy, Spain and South America. Today, more rice is eaten than any other grain.

Brown rice has seven layers, each of which contains protein, minerals, vitamins and fats which are important for the health of your body. When rice is processed or refined to make white rice the outer layers are removed and the goodness taken away. So try and master the art of cooking brown rice really well by carefully following the instructions in the following two recipes.

Australian and Surinam long grain rice is thin, light and quick to cook. Italian short grain rice is more chewy and takes longer to cook. It is delicious in recipes such as Risotto or Baked Rice.

'Saffron' Rice with Almonds and Sweetcorn
(Serves 4)

You will need a medium-sized saucepan with a tight lid, a wooden spoon, a sieve and a small, thick frying pan to toast the almonds in.

Imperial (Metric)	American
8 oz (225g) Surinam or Australian long grain brown rice	I cup Surinam or Australian long grain brown rice
3 tablespoons corn or sunflower oil	3 tablespoons corn or sunflower oil
I large onion, chopped	I large onion, chopped
I level teaspoon turmeric	I level teaspoon turmeric
I pint (575ml) hot water	2½ cups hot water
I level teaspoon sea salt	I level teaspoon sea salt
4 oz (110g) frozen sweetcorn	⅔ cup frozen sweetcorn
4 oz (110g) frozen peas	⅔ cup frozen peas
I teaspoon sunflower oil	I teaspoon sunflower oil
4 oz (110g) split almonds	I cup split almonds
I teaspoon lemon juice	I teaspoon lemon juice
I tablespoon shoyu	I tablespoon shoyu
I tablespoon fresh chopped parsley	I tablespoon fresh chopped parsley

1 Put the rice in the sieve and wash thoroughly with cold water for 1 minute. Leave to drain.

2 Heat the oil in the saucepan and sauté the onion for 5 minutes, until soft. Do not allow to burn.

3 Stir in the turmeric. Stir and heat for 1 minute more. This is slightly spicy and will turn the rice yellow.

4 Sprinkle in the drained rice and cook on a low heat for 4 minutes, stirring with a wooden spoon to coat the rice well.

5 Now add the hot water and sea salt.

6 Bring to the boil. Stir and turn heat down so that the rice is just bubbling gently. Cover and simmer for 25 minutes.

7 While the rice is cooking put the sweetcorn and peas in a little boiling water and cook for 4 minutes only. Drain.

8 In the small frying pan toast the almonds in just 1 teaspoon oil. Keep heat low and stir with wooden spoon for 5 minutes until lightly brown.

9 When the rice mixture is cooked and all the water has been absorbed, lightly stir in the sweetcorn, peas, lemon juice, shoyu and *half* the almonds with a fork. Do not mash the ingredients.

10 Put into a warm serving dish, sprinkle on the other half of the almonds and the chopped parsley. Serve this with Tomato, Orange and Cucumber Platter (see page 67 for recipe) and your guests will be well fed.

Baked Risotto with Cashew Nuts
(Serves 4)

You will need a 10-inch (25cm) round ovenproof baking dish (no lid needed), a sieve, 1 medium-sized saucepan, a sharp knife and a wooden spoon.

Imperial (Metric)	American
8 oz (225g) Italian short grain brown rice	I cup Italian short grain brown rice
I pint (575ml) cold water	2½ cups cold water
I level teaspoon sea salt	I level teaspoon sea salt
2 tablespoons corn *or* sunflower oil	2 tablespoons corn *or* sunflower oil
I large onion, finely chopped	I large onion, finely chopped
2 carrots (about 6 oz/175g) cut into thin I-inch (2.5cm) sticks	2 carrots (about 6 ounces) cut into thin I-inch sticks
I rounded teaspoon basil	I rounded teaspoon basil
½ level teaspoon tarragon (optional)	½ level teaspoon tarragon (optional)
3 oz (75g) cashew nuts	¾ cup cashew nuts
14 oz (400g) tin tomatoes, chopped	14 ounce can tomatoes, chopped
I tablespoon shoyu	I tablespoon shoyu
3 oz (75g) grated Cheddar cheese	¾ cup grated Cheddar cheese

1 Put the rice in the sieve and wash thoroughly with cold water for 1 minute. Drain.

2 Put the water, rice and sea salt in the saucepan. Bring to the boil. Turn down the heat so that the rice is just bubbling. Cover and simmer for 30 minutes.

3 While the rice is cooking heat the oil and fry the onion and carrots for 7 minutes. Do not allow to burn.

4 Sprinkle on the basil, tarragon and cashew nuts and stir well together.

5 Add the chopped tomatoes. Heat through and cook for 1 minute. Stir in shoyu.

6 When the rice is cooked it will have soaked up all the water. If there is any liquid left, just drain through the sieve.

7 Put the rice and vegetable mixture into a baking dish and mix all together lightly with a fork.

8 Sprinkle the grated cheese on top and add a little more basil if you like.

9 Bake in the oven at 375°F/190°C (Gas Mark 5) for 30 minutes. Serve with Shades of Green Salad (see page 66 for this recipe).

Millet

I know what some of you are thinking. Well, millet is not just for the birds, we deserve it too. This lovely grain is used in many parts of Africa, India and Asia. It is the main grain eaten by the Hunzas, a tribe who live in the foothills of the Himalayas. They are famous for very good health and living unusually long lives. They also eat whole wheat, yogurt, meat (only once or twice weekly), and plenty of fresh fruit, particularly apricots, and fresh vegetables.

In the two recipes here for you to try I use wholegrain millet and millet flakes, both of which can be bought at most wholefood or health food shops.

Millet Bake

You will need a frying pan, a casserole dish with a lid, a wooden spoon, a fork and a sharp knife.

Imperial (Metric)	American
3 tablespoons corn or sunflower oil	3 tablespoons corn or sunflower oil
8 oz (225g) wholegrain millet	I cup wholegrain millet
I large onion, finely chopped	I large onion, finely chopped
I large or 2 medium carrots, finely chopped	I large or 2 medium carrots, finely chopped
4 oz (110g) small button mushrooms, sliced	I cup small button mushrooms, sliced
I tablespoon fresh parsley, finely chopped	I tablespoon fresh parsley, finely chopped
I tablespoon lemon thyme or marjoram	I tablespoon lemon thyme or marjoram
Freshly ground black pepper	Freshly ground black pepper
I½ pints (850ml) vegetable stock	3¾ cups vegetable stock
2 medium tomatoes, thinly sliced in rings	2 medium tomatoes, thinly sliced in rings
4 oz (110g) grated Cheddar cheese	I cup grated Cheddar cheese

1 Put 1 tablespoon of oil in a frying pan. Heat and add the dry millet.

2 Stir and cook over low heat until the millet is very lightly toasted. This takes about 5 minutes. Put the millet into a baking dish.

3 Put the rest of the oil in a frying pan. Heat and add the onions and carrots. Fry gently for 5 minutes;

4 Add the mushrooms and fry for 2 minutes more.

5 Stir in the parsley and marjoram or lemon thyme.

6 Add this vegetable mixture to the millet, plus a little black pepper.

7 Now add the hot stock. Stir with a fork and float the tomato rings on top.

8 Now sprinkle the grated cheese and marjoram on top. Put lid on and bake in the centre of the oven, 350°F/180°C (Gas Mark 4) for 1 hour.

Part II — Beans

All dried beans, peas and lentils come under the general name of pulses. They are a good source of protein and are rich in vitamins and minerals.

Protein contains substances called amino acids. These amino acids are needed by our bodies to build complete protein. Some protein foods, such as soya beans, meat, eggs, cheese and fish, have all the important amino acids in them, while other protein foods have only some of the necessary acids. Except for the soya bean, all pulses have some of the needed amino acids missing. So the thing to do is eat pulses with other protein foods that have the missing acids in them.

If you eat beans, peas or lentils with wholegrains such as whole wheat, brown rice or millet, you are providing your body with a complete protein. Baked beans on wholemeal toast is a complete protein, for example. Also, adding cheese or nuts and seeds to your bean recipes will give you a complete protein. So there is no need to worry about not getting the right amount of protein or vitamins and minerals when you learn to balance the food you eat.

Another important thing to remember is that if we eat more pulses and whole grains and less meat, not only will we be healthier, but we will be helping the earth to feed more people. To grow these crops costs only 10 per cent of the total cost of feeding the animals that will eventually be our meat.

'Pass the beans, please' and follow my cooking instructions and you won't get indigestion.

Aduki Beans: These little red beans have a grand title in Japan. They are called 'The King of Beans' and have been cultivated and eaten there and in China for many centuries. Not only are they eaten as a food but the juice from the cooked bean is used as a medicine and is believed to help cure kidney problems. These beans sprout very well, too (see page 70 on sprouting your own seeds and beans).

Aduki Bean Rissoles
(Makes 8)

You will need a frying pan, a saucepan, a mixing bowl and a sieve.

Imperial (Metric)	American
6 oz (175g) aduki beans, soaked in cold water overnight	¾ cup aduki beans, soaked in cold water overnight
6 oz (175g) porridge oats	1½ cup rolled oats
1 medium onion, very finely chopped	1 medium onion, very finely chopped
2 tablespoon fresh chopped parsley	2 tablespoons fresh chopped parsley
1 teaspoon basil	1 teaspoon basil
2 tablespoons tomatoe purée	2 tablespoons tomato paste
2 tablespoons shoyu	2 tablespoons shoyu
1 egg, beaten	1 egg, beaten
Freshly ground black pepper	Freshly ground black pepper
Corn or sunflower oil for frying	Corn or sunflower oil for frying

1 Rinse the soaked beans well by putting them in a sieve and letting cold water run over them.

2 Put the beans in the saucepan with cold water and *no salt* or your beans will not soften properly.

3 Bring the water to boil and turn down to simmer. Simmer with the lid on for 35 to 40 minutes until beans are soft but not too mushy.

4 Drain off water and put the beans into a mixing bowl.

5 Add all other ingredients except for 2 oz (50g/½ cup) of oats. Mix well together with a fork and then your hands.

6 Form in round rissole shapes about ½ inch (1cm) thick. You should have 8 good sized rissoles.

7 Dip each one in the remaining oats.

8 Put a little oil in the frying pan and fry the rissoles on medium heat for 4 minutes on each side. Do not allow to burn.

Note: These rissoles are delicious with Real Tomato Ketchup (see page 30 for the recipe) and any simple salad for lunch-time or, for a hot main meal, make a simple gravy and serve with baked jacket potatoes and steamed cauliflower.

Butter (Lima) Bean Pie

You will need a casserole dish without a lid, a saucepan, a sieve and a cheese grater.

For the filling:

Imperial (Metric)	American
8 oz (225g) butter beans, soaked overnight in 1½ pints (850ml) cold water	1⅓ cups lima beans, soaked overnight in 3¾ cups cold water
2 tablespoons corn or sunflower oil	2 tablespoons corn or sunflower oil
1 large onion, finely chopped	1 large onion, finely chopped
2 sticks celery, finely chopped	2 stalks celery, finely chopped
1 teaspoon mixed herbs	1 teaspoon mixed herbs
2 tablespoons tomato purée	2 tablespoon tomato paste
1 vegetable stock cube	1 vegetable stock cube
Freshly ground black pepper	Freshly ground black pepper

For the topping:

Imperial (Metric)	American
4 large boiled potatoes with skins on	4 large boiled potatoes with skins on
3 oz (75g) grated Cheddar cheese	¾ cup grated Cheddar cheese

1 Rinse the soaked beans thoroughly by putting in a sieve and letting cold water run over them.

2 Put the beans in saucepan with 1¼ pints (700ml/3¼ cups) cold water but no salt. Bring to the boil, then turn down to simmer. Cover and cook gently for 45 minutes until the beans are soft.

3 Fry the onion in oil for 5 minutes. Add the celery and fry for 5 more minutes. Add the herbs and tomato purée (paste).

4 When the beans are cooked, add a stock cube to the beans and cooking water.

5 Pour the beans and cooking water into the casserole dish.

6 Stir in the onion mixture and add little freshly ground black pepper if you like.

7 For the topping, thinly slice the four cooked potatoes into rounds. Place these, overlapping each other, all over the top of the bean mixture.

8 Sprinkle the grated cheese over this and bake in the oven at 375°F/190°C (Gas Mark 5) for 30 minutes or until the top is golden-brown. Serve with Coleslaw Salad (see page 65 for salad ideas).

Mung Beans

These tiny green beans are what the Chinese use when sprouting beans. You can sprout your own — see page 70 on how to do this. You can also use them in soups instead of lentils or in this next recipe for a delicious Shepherd's Pie.

Mung Bean Shepherd's Pie
(Serves 4)

In this recipe I have used beef flavoured tvp soya mince, with mung beans. For more information on tvp (which means texturized vegetable protein) see page 50 and you will find out why it is so useful.

You will need a casserole dish, a saucepan, a frying pan, a sharp knife and a sieve.

For the filling:

Imperial (Metric)	American
6 oz (175g) mung beans soaked in 1¼ pints (700ml) cold water for 4 hours	I cup mung beans soaked in 3¼ cups cold water for 4 hours
1½ oz (38g) tvp soya mince, beef flavoured	¼ cup tvp soy mince, beef flavoured
I large onion, finely chopped	I large onion, finely chopped
2 large carrots, scraped and chopped into small pieces	2 large carrots, scraped and chopped into small pieces
2 tablespoons corn or sunflower oil	2 tablespoons corn or sunflower oil
I bay leaf	I bay leaf
I teaspoon basil	I teaspoon basil
2 tablespoons tomato purée	2 tablespoons tomato paste
I tablespoon shoyu	I tablespoon shoyu
I tablespoon fresh chopped parsley	I tablespoon freshly chopped parsley
Sea salt and freshly ground black pepper	Sea salt and freshly ground black pepper

For the topping:

Imperial (Metric)	American
2 lbs (900g) cooked mashed potatoes	4 cups cooked mashed potato
3 tablespoons natural yogurt or milk	3 tablespoons plain yogurt or milk
1 oz butter or margarine	2 tablespoons butter or margarine
1 tomato, thinly sliced	1 tomato, thinly sliced
2 oz (50g) Cheddar cheese grated	½ cup grated Cheddar cheese

1 Rinse the soaked mung beans by putting them in a sieve and letting cold water run over them.

2 Put the beans in a saucepan with 1 pint (575ml/2½ cups) cold water (no salt, or the beans will not soften enough).

3 Bring to the boil. Turn down to simmer, cover and let cook gently for 30 mins.

4 Pour enough boiling water over the tvp mince to just cover it. Let it stand for 5 minutes.

5 While the beans are cooking, fry the onion and carrots in the oil for 7 minutes on medium heat.

6 Add the soya mince, bay leaf and basil. Fry this gently for 3 minutes. Do not burn.

7 Add tomato purée (paste), shoyu and parsley. Stir in well and fry for just 1 minute on a low heat.

8 When the beans are cooked pour them, with their cooking water, into the casserole dish, add the vegetable mixture and stir well in.

9 Taste and add a little sea salt and freshly ground black pepper if you like.

For the topping:

1 To the mashed potato, add the yogurt and butter or margarine plus a little sea salt if needed.

2 Spread the potato mixture over the mung bean mixture. Ridge the top with a fork. Place slices of tomato on top and sprinkle the grated cheese over this. Bake in the oven at 375°F/190°C (Gas Mark 5) for 30 minutes until golden-brown.

Part III — Nuts and Seeds

Nuts are not just a Christmas treat to crack open with the nutcracker, as is often the case in many homes. They are high in protein, and rich in minerals and vitamin B. You can obtain a fresh assorted variety of shelled nuts and seeds in health food or wholefood shops and make delicious savoury meals with them, and also pop them in cakes and biscuits to add that extra goodness. See Chapter 6 for ideas on baking with them.

Seeds such as *sunflower, sesame* and *pumpkin* are bursting with goodness in the way of vitamins and minerals. Those tiny gerbils and hamsters are onto a good thing when they are showered with those lovely striped sunflower seeds, but thank goodness you can buy these shelled or you would be picking away all day to get just a small handful. Sesame and sunflower seeds are also cheap and well worth learning to cook with. If you haven't tried American Granola (Toasted Malted Muesli, recipe on page 12) then now is your chance. It's fantastic! More recipes using seeds can be found in Chapter 6, Tea-time.

Now for a recipe which will make nut burgers or a Sunday nut roast.

Nut Burgers
(Makes 8)

These are really easy to make. You will need a liquidizer or the cheese grating attachment for a hand mincing machine to grind the nuts and grate the bread into crumbs. You will also need a mixing bowl and a frying pan.

Imperial (Metric)	American
8 oz (225g) mixed nuts and seeds	1½ cups mixed nuts and seeds
4 oz (110g) wholemeal breadcrumbs	2 cups wholewheat breadcrumbs
1 medium onion, finely chopped	1 medium onion, finely chopped
2 tablespoons fresh chopped parsley	2 tablespoons fresh chopped parsley
2 tablespoons corn or sunflower oil	2 tablespoons corn or sunflower oil
1½ tablespoons shoyu	1½ tablespoons shoyu
1 large egg	1 large egg
Sesame seeds for coating burgers	Sesame seeds for coating burgers
Vegetable oil for frying	Vegetable oil for frying

1 Grind the nuts and seeds, not too fine or coarse.

2 Put all the nut burger ingredients into a bowl. Mix with a fork and then press together with your hands. The mixture should be firm but not too stiff.

3 Form into 8 round burgers ½ inch (1cm) thick.

4 Dip the burgers into the sesame seeds, coating top and bottom.

5 Fry gently in oil about ¼ inch (5mm) deep for 4 minutes on each side. Take care not to burn.

Note: Almonds, cashews, peanuts and sunflower seeds make a good combination, but experiment to find your own favourites and add variety.

Part IV - Potatoes

Potatoes are a good, healthy food which can be made into many delicious and easy meals.

They are best baked or steamed with their jackets on because this method of cooking helps to retain the vitamins, especially vitamin C, and minerals.

Of course, you will have to take the skins off for mashed potatoes but if you follow my instructions for making creamy mashed potatoes you will not lose much of the goodness which lies just underneath the skin.

The next three recipes which are for mashed potatoes, chips and jacket potatoes, will no doubt be quite familiar to you, but as they are so often cooked extremely badly I have included them.

Creamy Mashed Potatoes
(4 portions)

Mashed potatoes are great for topping your Shepherd's Pie or serving with Nut Burgers. Use small or medium-sized potatoes as they will steam quicker.

If you do not have a steamer you will need an 8-inch (20cm) wide saucepan and a metal colander, as well as a fork or a potato masher.

Imperial (Metric)	American
2 lbs (900g) potatoes, scrubbed	2 pounds potatoes, scrubbed
2 tablespoons natural yogurt	2 tablespoons plain yogurt
1 tablespoon polyunsaturated margarine *or* butter	1 tablespoon polyunsaturated margarine *or* butter
Sea salt	Sea salt
Freshly ground black pepper	Freshly ground black pepper
A little fresh chopped parsley to serve	A little fresh chopped parsley to serve

1 If you do not have a steamer, half fill the saucepan with water. Place the colander on top, making sure all the holes in the colander are inside the pan.

2 Put the potatoes into the colander and cover them with the saucepan lid.

3 Bring the water to boil and let it simmer for 20 to 30 minutes until the potatoes are soft right through to the centre. You can test this with a skewer or knife.

4 When cooked, lift each one out with a fork and peel off the very thin skin.

5 Mash the potatoes with the yogurt, margarine or butter, sea salt and freshly ground black pepper.

6 Put in a warm serving bowl and sprinkle on the fresh parsley.

Note: To make cheesy mashed potatoes, just mash in 2 oz (50g/½ cup) grated Cheddar cheese.

Perfect Chips
(4 portions)

To make really perfect chips that are crisp on the outside and soft and light in the middle is not a very difficult task.

You will need a chip pan with a basket inside, a sharp knife and a clean tea towel. Wrapping the cut potatoes in the towel will dry out some of the moisture and make your chips crisper.

Imperial (Metric)	American
3 potatoes, weight about 6 oz (175g) each	3 potatoes, weighing about 6 ounces each
Soya or corn oil for deep frying	Soya or corn oil for deep frying

1 Scrub the potatoes (*leave skins on*).

2 Slice into chip shapes. The length will vary but make sure they are no wider than ½ inch (1cm).

3 Wrap the cut chips in a clean tea towel.

4 Take out the basket from the chip pan and heat the oil to very hot (make sure the pan is on the back ring of the stove).

5 Put the chips into the basket and lower gently into the hot oil.

6 Cook the chips in hot oil until golden-brown.

7 Lift the basket out carefully and drain the chips on kitchen paper.

Jacket Potatoes

You can create so many different meals with a simple baked jacket potato. I will give you a few ideas on stuffing baked potatoes but it is very important to learn to bake your potatoes well first. I have eaten the most awful jacket potatoes which had brittle hard skins and mushy or soapy-hard centres so don't just throw your potatoes in the oven and hope for the best. Try this way for prize-winning jacket potatoes.

Imperial (Metric)	American
4 potatoes, weighing 6-8 oz/175-225g each	4 potatoes weighing 6-8 ounces each
2 teaspoons corn or sunflower oil	2 teaspoons corn or sunflower oil
Large pinch of sea salt	Large pinch of sea salt

1 Heat the oven to 400°F/200°C (Gas Mark 6).

2 Scrub the potatoes. Wipe dry. Pierce each one with a skewer through the centre, and remove the skewer.

3 Cut a thin slit all round each potato as if you were going to cut it in half.

4 Put the oil and salt in a cereal bowl.

5 Rub each potato with the oil and salt mixture.

6 Bake in the centre of the oven for 40 minutes to 1 hour, depending on the size of the potato. Test with a skewer or a knife to see if the centre is soft.

7 Slice open potatoes and either serve them with a little butter or polyunsaturated margarine, sea salt and freshly ground black pepper, *or* cottage cheese with a few chopped chives and a pinch of sea salt on top. Or stuff them according to one of the following recipes.

Stuffed Baked Potatoes: Filling I

Imperial (Metric)	American
4 jacket potatoes, cooked	4 jacket potatoes, cooked
2 tablespoons natural yogurt	2 tablespoons plain yogurt
I small onion, finely chopped	I small onion, finely chopped
2 oz (50g) finely ground sunflower seeds *or* nuts	½ cup finely ground sunflower seeds *or* nuts
2 tablespoons fresh chopped parsley	2 tablespoons fresh chopped parsley
3 oz (75g) grated Cheddar cheese	¾ cup grated Cheddar cheese
Salt and freshly ground black pepper, to taste	Salt and freshly ground black pepper, to taste

1 Cut the cooked potatoes in half.

2 Scoop out the insides.

3 Mash all the ingredients together in a bowl, reserving 1 oz (25g/¼ cup) of cheese.

4 Spoon the mixture back into the skins. Sprinkle the remaining cheese on the top.

5 Bake in the oven for 10 minutes and then grill (broil) for 2 minutes until golden-brown on top. Serve with a coleslaw salad for truly satisfying meal.

Stuffed Baked Potatoes: Filling II

Very similar to Filling I, but takes a little longer to prepare.

Imperial (Metric)	American
1 oz (25g) soya mince, beef flavoured	¼ cup tvp soy mince, beef flavoured
3 tablespoons finely chopped onion	3 tablespoons finely chopped onion
1 tablespoon corn or sunflower oil	1 tablespoon corn or sunflower oil
4 jacket potatoes, cooked	4 jacket potatoes, cooked
3 oz (75g) grated Cheddar cheese	¾ cup grated Cheddar cheese
3 tablespoons natural yogurt	3 tablespoons plain yogurt
2 tablespoons fresh chopped parsley	2 tablespoons fresh chopped parsley

1 Place the tvp mince in a cup and pour boiling water over it. This will reconstitute it, that is, it will swell to its original size. Leave to stand for 5 to 10 minutes.

2 Fry the onion in the oil for 5 minutes until soft.

3 Add the soya mince. Drain away any water that has not been soaked up.

4 Fry the onion and mince for 5 minutes.

5 Cut the cooked potatoes in half. Scoop out the middle. Mix in all the ingredients, but leave 1 oz (25g/¼cup) of cheese for the top.

6 Spoon the mixture into the jackets.

7 Sprinkle a little cheese on top.

8 Bake for 10 minutes then grill (broil) until golden-brown.

Potato Scallops
(Serves 4)

This is a favourite lunch-time tummy-filler. You will need a 3 inch (7cm) high ovenproof dish, an egg whisk and a cheese grater.

Imperial (Metric)	American
1 large clove garlic (optional)	1 large clove garlic (optional)
1 oz (25g) butter or polyunsaturated margarine	2 tablespoons butter or polyunsaturated margarine
Sea salt, freshly ground black pepper and a little grated nutmeg	Sea salt, freshly ground black pepper and a little grated nutmeg
1 lb (450g) potatoes, scrubbed (not peeled)	1 pound potatoes, scrubbed (not peeled)
4 oz (110g) grated Cheddar cheese	1 cup grated Cheddar cheese
2 eggs	2 eggs
2 fl oz (60ml) milk, just warm	¼ cup milk, just warm

1 Set the oven to 375°F/190°C (Gas Mark 5).

2 Crush the garlic. If you do not have a garlic crusher just chop finely then press the garlic clove with the side of the knife until it is soft and juicy.

3 Spread a little polyunsaturated margarine or butter all over the dish then spread the garlic over the bottom of the dish.

4 Slice the potatoes very thinly and arrange them in overlapping rows in the dish, sprinkling each layer of potatoes with a little sea salt, freshly ground black pepper and nutmeg.

5 On the top layer sprinkle on the cheese and dots of margarine *or* butter.

6 Beat the eggs and and then mix with the warm milk.

7 Pour this over the potatoes. It should only just cover them.

8 Bake in the oven for 1 hour or until crisp on top and soft in the middle.

Part V — Tvp (Texturized Vegetable Protein) and Wholemeal Pasta Dishes

About Tvp

You can buy tvp mince or chunks in several different meat-like flavours. It is made from soya bean flour and is a dried food which has to be reconstituted before you use it in your recipes. This simply means that you add about 2½ times its weight in hot water. Chunks are best soaked for 2 or more hours, while the mince needs only 10 minutes to swell up to its original size.

Tvp is a complete protein food, equal to the protein contained in meat once you have reconstituted it. So, if a recipe calls for 1 lb (455g)/2 cups) mince then you will only need about 5 oz (130g/1 cup) of dried tvp mince to give you the same amount of protein.

Two very good reasons for learning to use tvp are that it is a quarter the price of most meat and that ten times more land is needed to breed animals for the meat market than to grow vegetable protein such as the soya bean.

The following recipe is my version of the Italian Bolognese Sauce. It is quite delicious and has many uses. It is mainly eaten with spaghetti but I love it, too, in savoury pancakes with a white sauce or mixed with brown rice to make a really tasty risotto. Two cups of cooked brown rice (see page 34 for recipe) and one cup left-over Bolognese Sauce makes this marvellous, quick supper dish.

Bolognese Sauce
(Serves 4)

You will need a medium-sized thick saucepan with a lid, and a wooden spoon. It is not essential, but a vegetable chopper would be useful to cut the vegetables very finely although a sharp knife will do.

Imperial (Metric)	American
2 oz (50g) soya (tvp) mince, beef flavoured	½ cup soy (tvp) mince, beef flavoured
4 fl oz (120ml) hot water	½ cup hot water
2 tablespoons corn or sunflower oil	2 tablespoons corn or sunflower oil
I large onion (8 oz/225g in weight), very finely chopped	I large onion (8 ounces in weight) very finely chopped
I large clove garlic, crushed	I large clove garlic, crushed
2 sticks celery, very finely chopped	2 stalks celery, very finely chopped
½ green pepper, very finely chopped	½ green pepper, very finely chopped
I level teaspoon basil	I level teaspoon basil
I small bay leaf	I small bay leaf
2 oz (50g) finely chopped almonds and hazelnuts	½ cup finely chopped almonds or filberts
14 oz (400g) tin tomatoes, chopped	14 ounce can tomatoes, chopped
I tablespoon tomato purée	I tablespoon tomato paste
Sea salt and freshly ground black pepper, to taste	Sea salt and freshly ground black pepper, to taste
I tablespoon lemon juice	I tablespoon lemon juice

1 Pour the hot water over the soya mince and let stand for 10 minutes.

2 Heat oil and fry onion, garlic and celery for 10 minutes on low heat with lid on.

3 Squeeze the mince gently of excess water and add to pan stirring it in well with the cooking vegetables.

4 Add the green pepper, basil, bay leaf and nuts.

5 Stir well in together and fry for 2 minutes on medium heat.

6 Add the tomatoes and purée (paste).

7 Stir well in and taste. Now add a little sea salt and pepper if you like. (Note: you could add ½ vegetable stock cube instead of salt if you like.)

8 Let mixture simmer gently for 30 minutes on low heat with lid on. When cooked, add the lemon juice.

Different ways to serve Bolognese Sauce:

Spaghetti Bolognese
(Serves 4)

Choose wholewheat spaghetti as this is made with wholemeal flour and not a refined white flour. You will need a large saucepan and a fork.

Imperial (Metric)	American
I quantity Bolognese Sauce (see page 50)	I quantity Bolognese Sauce (see page 50)
8 oz (225g) long thin wholewheat spaghetti	8 ounces long thin wholewheat spaghetti
2 pints (1.15 litres) boiling water	5 cups boiling water
I tablespoon corn *or* sunflower oil	I tablespoon corn *or* sunflower oil
I teaspoon sea salt	I teaspoon sea salt
4 oz (110g) grated Cheddar cheese	I cup grated Cheddar cheese

1 Add the oil and salt to the boiling water.

2 Gently curve in the long spaghetti and stir with a fork to separate the strands. Boil for 15 minutes.

3 Gently heat your Bolognese Sauce.

4 When the spaghetti is cooked, place into a colander and sprinkle on a little oil to stop the strands sticking.

5 Serve onto hot dinner plates and spoon a soup ladle full of Bolognese Sauce on top of each mound. Serve with a little grated cheese and Shades of Green Salad (see page 66 for recipe) and you will have created a truly balanced meal.

Bolognese Stuffed Savoury Pancakes
(Serves 4 to 5)

These are really delicious, but quite a lot of preparation is needed so make them for very special occasions.

You will need a small, thick frying pan, a piece of kitchen paper or tissue screwed up into a ball plus 1 teaspoon corn or sunflower oil in a dish ready to lightly grease your pan. You will also need a fish slice or a palette knife, a mixing bowl, a fork, a tablespoon and a large square 2 inch (5cm) deep ovenproof dish.

For the pancakes:

Imperial (Metric)	American
4 oz (110g) wholemeal flour	I cup wholewheat flour
½ teaspoon sea salt	½ teaspoon sea salt
½ teaspoon bicarbonate of soda	½ teaspoon baking soda
I large egg	I large egg
8 fl oz (250ml) milk	I cup milk
Vegetable oil for frying	Vegetable oil for frying

1 Put flour, sea salt and bicarbonate of soda (baking soda) in a bowl. Make a well in the middle.

2 Break in egg and add half the milk. Mix well with a fork and gradually add the remaining milk.

3 Leave to stand, covered with a plate for 15 minutes.

4 Stir again. Your batter is now ready for use.

5 Spread a little oil around the pan with the kitchen paper which you have dipped in the oil. Heat the pan on medium to high heat and put 2 tablespoons of the mixture in the centre.

6 Lift pan off heat and tilt it so that the mixture spreads out thinly, then replace the pan on the heat.

7 When bubbles show on top turn pancake over with a fish slice and cook quickly on the other side for about 30 seconds.

8 Repeat, not forgetting to oil pan lightly before cooking each pancake. Pile on top of each other (they will not stick) and set aside.

For the Light Cheese Sauce:

Imperial (Metric)	American
I pint (575ml) milk	2½ cups milk
1½ oz (40g) 81-85 per cent wholemeal flour	¼ cup 81-85 per cent wholewheat flour
I very level teaspoon sea salt	I very level teaspoon sea salt
½ teaspoon freshly ground black pepper	½ teaspoon freshly ground black pepper
2 oz (50g) grated Cheddar cheese	½ cup grated Cheddar cheese

1 Pour ¼ pint (140ml/⅔ cup) milk into a small mixing bowl with the flour. Mix well together with a fork.

2 Bring the rest of the milk to the boil. *Take off the heat.*

3 Add a little of the hot milk to the flour mixture and stir to smooth paste.

4 Add this paste to the saucepan of hot milk, stirring all the time. Bring to the boil on low heat, still stirring. Add sea salt and freshly ground black pepper.

5 Simmer for 5 minutes, then remove from the heat.

6 Add the cheese and stir in well.

To prepare the dish:

Imperial (Metric)	American
I quantity Bolognese Sauce (page 50)	I quantity Bolognese Sauce (page 50)
2 oz (50g) grated Cheddar cheese	½ cup grated Cheddar cheese

1 Grease your ovenproof dish.

2 Place 2 tablespoons of the Bolognese Sauce along the centre of each pancake. Roll them up and arrange them in the dish.

3 Pour the white sauce over the top and sprinkle on the last remaining 2 oz (50g/½ cup) cheese.

4 Bake at 400°F/200°C (Gas Mark 6) for 20 minutes. The top should be golden brown, but do not overcook. If, after 20 minutes, the top is not golden-brown just grill (broil) for 1 minute. Serve with a fresh salad or lightly cooked runner (green) or French (snap) beans.

Macaroni Cheese

I don't think that I have ever eaten a meal more badly cooked than Macaroni Cheese. Dollops of glue-like mounds held together with a thick tasteless sauce is my childhood memory of this dish. Well it doesn't have to be like that — it can be scrumptious. I use wholewheat macaroni instead of the refined white type as it is made with wholemeal flour and, of course, more nutritious.

You will need a medium-sized thick saucepan, an 8 inch (20cm) casserole dish, a sharp knife, a wooden spoon, a fork and a colander.

For the Macaroni:

Imperial (Metric)	American
1½ pints (800ml) boiling water	3¾ cups boiling water
1 level teaspoon sea salt	1 level teaspoon sea salt
1 dessertspoon corn *or* sunflower oil	2 teaspoons corn *or* sunflower oil
6 oz (175g) wholewheat macaroni	1½ cups wholewheat macaroni

1 Into the boiling water put the salt and the oil, then stir in the macaroni with a fork.

2 Bring back to the boil and cook on medium heat for 15 minutes.

3 Drain well in a colander, shaking all the water out.

4 Place in the casserole dish and trickle oil onto the macaroni. Use a fork to move the macaroni around so that you coat it lightly with the oil. This stops it sticking while you make your sauce.

For the Sauce:

Imperial (Metric)	American
1 medium onion, very finely chopped	1 medium onion, very finely chopped
2 sticks celery, very finely chopped	2 stalks celery, very finely chopped
2 oz (50g) button mushrooms, sliced (optional)	1 cup button mushrooms sliced (optional)
1 tablespoon red or green pepper, finely chopped (optional)	1 tablespoon red or green pepper, finely chopped (optional)
1¼ pints (700ml) milk	3¼ cups milk
1½ oz (40g) 81 or 85 per cent wholemeal flour	⅓ cup 81 or 85 per cent wholewheat flour
1 level teaspoon sea salt	1 level teaspoon sea salt
¼ teaspoon freshly ground black pepper (optional)	¼ teaspoon freshly ground black pepper (optional)
5 oz (150g) grated Cheddar cheese	1¼ cups grated Cheddar cheese

1 Heat the oil in the saucepan and fry the onions and celery on low heat for 6 minutes. Keep covered.

2 Add the mushrooms and peppers, if you are using them. Fry for another 3 minutes only. Then pour in 1 pint (575ml/2½ cups) of the milk.

3 While this is slowly heating, put the flour in a small bowl and, with a fork, mix in the remaining milk. Mix to a smooth, runny paste.

4 The milk in the saucepan should now be hot. *Remove from the heat.* Strain a little of this onto the flour paste.

5 Stir well together then pour into the saucepan, stirring all the time with a wooden spoon.

6 Place saucepan back on the heat and bring slowly to boil stirring well. Turn down heat and let simmer for 5 minutes only. Add the sea salt and freshly ground black pepper.

7 When the sauce is thickened and cooked add 4 oz (110g/1 cup) of the cheese.

8 Pour the sauce over the macaroni. Use a fork to mix it carefully together.

9 Sprinkle the remaining 2 oz (50g/½ cup) of cheese on top. Bake at 375°F/190°C (Gas Mark 5) for 20 minutes, until the top is golden-brown. Do not overcook. If the top is not brown after 20 minutes, grill (broil) to brown lightly.

Part VI — Wholemeal Shortcrust Pastry

Using whole grain flour in pastry making is slightly more difficult than using white flour, but once you have mastered the knack you will have no problems. I have experimented a great deal to find a method that turns out perfect pastry every time.

The method I use, which is quite different from the traditional 'rubbing in' method, releases the gluten (which is the protein) in the flour and helps to lighten your pastry enormously.

Note: When making *Puff* or *Flaky* Pastry I always use 81 per cent wholemeal flour as the 100 per cent wholemeal is too heavy, but for Shortcrust Pastry 100 per cent wholemeal flour is perfect. So have a go with the following recipes and you will be pleasantly surprised at how much tastier your pastry is.

Basic Wholemeal Shortcrust Pastry
(Enough to line an 8 inch/20cm flan dish)

You will need a mixing bowl, a fork, a plastic bag to put the pastry in, a plate and a palette knife. Read the method before you start as mine is not the traditional way of making pastry.

Imperial (Metric)	American
6 oz (175g) wholemeal flour	1½ cups wholewheat flour
Good pinch of sea salt	Good pinch of sea salt
Scant 2 tablespoons cold water	Scant 2 tablespoons cold water
3 oz (80g) polyunsaturated margarine	6 tablespoons polyunsaturated margarine

1 Mix the flour and sea salt and put on a plate.

2 Put the margarine, water and 1 heaped tablespoon of the flour in the mixing bowl.

3 Cream together with a fork or wooden spoon.

4 Gradually add the rest of the flour.

5 Using your hands, press mixture well together to form a softish dough. Knead this for 1 minute.

6 Put the dough in the plastic bag, flatten it and place in the fridge for 20 minutes or the freezer for 5 minutes.

7 Your pastry is now ready to roll out. Flour a clean surface and roll the dough out. To lift off the surface use a palette knife near one edge, lift the edge of the pastry onto the rolling pin, curl it around the pin and lift it onto your greased flan dish or on top of a filling, depending on what you are making.

Here are a few recipes that will be well-loved and satisfying using your wholemeal pastry.

Tomato Quiche
(6 portions)

You will need a 8 inch (20cm) flan dish, an egg whisk and a jug.

Imperial (Metric)	American
I quantity wholemeal pastry (page 57)	I quantity wholewheat pastry (page 57)
3 eggs	3 eggs
¼ pint (140ml) milk	⅔ cup milk
2 tablespoons thick natural yogurt	2 tablespoons thick plain yogurt
I tablespoon dried skimmed milk powder	I tablespoon dried skimmed milk powder
¼ level teaspoon freshly ground black pepper	¼ level teaspoon freshly ground black pepper
½ level teaspoon sea salt	½ level teaspoon sea salt
¼ teaspoon ground mace or nutmeg	¼ teaspoon ground mace or nutmeg
4 oz (110g) grated Cheddar Cheese	I cup grated Cheddar cheese
I tablespoon onion, *very* finely chopped	I tablespoon onion, *very* finely chopped
7 slices of tomato	7 slices of tomato
I level teaspoon oregano	I level teaspoon oregano

1 Set the oven to 375°F/190°C (Gas Mark 5).

2 Roll out the pastry as directed on page 57 and line your flan dish. Prick the bottom with a fork in eight places. Bake in the oven for 10 minutes.

3 Whisk the eggs, milk, yogurt, powdered milk, freshly ground black pepper, sea salt and mace together.

4 When the pastry case has been baked for 10 minutes, sprinkle a little cheese on the bottom.

5 Then spread onion over the cheese. Cover this with more cheese, reserving a little for the top.

6 Place the tomato slices all around the edge plus one slice in the middle.

7 Put the egg mixture into a jug and pour evenly over the tomatoes.

8 Sprinkle on the remaining grated cheese and the oregano. Bake for 35 to 40 minutes. Let it stand for 10 minutes before serving.

Soya (Soy) Chunk Steak Pie

Using only 3 ounces (75g) soya (soy) chunks will give you the same protein as 12 ounces (375g) of beef steak at a quarter of the cost. Follow the instructions carefully and the flavour of your pie filling will be quite delicious. *Soak* the chunks *overnight*, or for at least 2 hours, in 1 pint (575ml/2½ cups) water. You will need a 10 inch (25cm) round, square or oval pie dish, well greased, a medium-sized saucepan, a sharp knife, a wooden spoon and a pastry brush.

For the Pastry:

Imperial (Metric)	American
8 oz (225g) wholemeal flour	2 cups wholewheat flour
I very level teaspoon baking powder	I very level teaspoon baking powder
4 oz (110g) polyunsaturated margarine	½ cup polyunsaturated margarine
3 tablespoons cold water	3 tablespoons cold water
Pinch of sea salt	Pinch of sea salt
A little beaten egg for glazing	A little beaten egg for glazing

For the Filling:

Imperial (Metric)	American
3 oz (75g) beef flavoured soya chunks	3 ounces beef flavoured soy chunks
I large onion, approx. 6 oz (175g) when peeled and chopped	I large onion, about I cup when peeled and chopped
I large clove garlic, crushed	I large clove garlic, crushed
6 oz (175g) scraped and chopped carrots	I cup scraped and chopped carrots
3 tablespoons corn *or* sunflower oil	3 tablespoons corn *or* sunflower oil
2 sticks celery chopped	2 stalks celery, chopped
I very small green pepper, chopped	I very small green pepper, chopped
I tablespoon 100 per cent wholemeal flour	I tablespoon 100 per cent wholewheat flour
I pint (575ml) light vegetable stock (using ½ stock cube only)	2½ cups light vegetable stock (using ½ stock cube only)
2 tablespoons fresh chopped parsley	2 tablespoons fresh chopped parsley
I generous teaspoon *sweet* mixed herbs or marjoram	I generous teaspoon *sweet* mixed herbs or marjoram
I heaped tablespoon tomato purée	I heaped tablespoon tomato paste
4 oz (110g) frozen peas	⅔ cup frozen peas
I tablespoon shoyu	I tablespoon shoyu

1 Make the pastry according to the instructions on page 57. Refrigerate, in a plastic bag, while you make the filling.

2 As directed above soak the chunks in water for at least 2 hours or, even better, overnight. Drain and discard water.

3 Fry the onion, garlic and carrots in the oil for 5 minutes. Add the celery and continue to sauté for another 3 minutes.

4 Add the tvp chunks and fry, stirring gently, for 3 minutes. Add the chopped pepper and continue frying for 1 minute.

5 Sprinkle on the flour, stirring all the time. Blend it well into the vegetables and chunks.

6 Add the hot stock, parsley, herbs and tomato purée (paste) stirring until smooth. Simmer on a low heat, covered, for 20 minutes.

7 Add the frozen peas and the shoyu, and remove from the heat immediately.

8 Pour filling into the pie dish. Let cook for 10 minutes.

9 Heat the oven to 350°F/190°C (Gas Mark 5).

10 Roll out pastry as directed on page 57. Lift it on to your rolling pin and place it on top of the pie filling.

11 Trim off, crimp and fork-pattern the edges, and make a few leaf shapes out of the pastry trimmings to decorate the top.

12 Stick on the leaves with a little egg wash, brush the pastry top with more egg wash and bake for 35 minutes. Serve with lightly steamed sprouts, spring greens or cauliflower.

Corn Fritters

To finish this Chapter, I will give you a very simple recipe that everyone seems to like. It is very nutritious and quick to prepare. Great for Saturday lunch when the shopping is done.

The soya (soy) flour adds extra protein but you can just use all wholemeal flour in the recipe instead.

You will need a sieve, mixing bowl, fork, a small, thick frying pan, a tablespoon and a fish slice or palette knife.

Imperial (Metric)	American
8 oz (225g) frozen sweetcorn	1⅓ cups frozen sweetcorn
3 oz (75g) wholemeal flour	¾ cup wholewheat flour
I oz soya flour	¼ cup soy flour
I level teaspoon baking powder	I level teaspoon baking powder
½ teaspoon sea salt	½ teaspoon sea salt
I large egg	I large egg
8 fl oz (250ml) milk	I cup milk
2 tablespoons very finely chopped onion (optional)	2 tablespoons very finely chopped onion (optional)
3 oz (75g) grated Cheddar cheese	¾ cup grated Cheddar cheese
Corn oil for frying	Corn oil for frying

1 Cook the sweetcorn in a little salted water for 4 minutes only. Leave to cool.

2 Put the wholemeal flour, soya (soy) flour, baking powder and salt in the sieve and shake into the mixing bowl.

3 Make a well in the middle of the dry ingredients and add the egg and half of the milk.

4 Blend well, gradually adding the remaining milk to make a smooth thick batter.

5 Add the onion, grated cheese and the cool sweetcorn.

6 Leave to stand for 15 minutes. Stir again. Your mixture is now ready.

7 Heat 2 tablespoons oil in the frying pan.

8 Each fritter will use 1 tablespoon of batter. You should be able to get three at a time in a pan. Gently spread each fritter flat with the back of the tablespoon.

9 Let them get crisp and golden brown on one side using moderately high heat for 2 minutes.

10 Lower the heat and turn the fritters over. Cook on the other side for 2 minutes until golden-brown.

Note: These will keep quite crisp in the oven but any pancake type mixture is always best eaten as soon as it is cooked. Don't forget to leave some batter for yourself because you will get lots of shouts for more!

I hope this chapter has given you lots of new ideas and ingredients to experiment with. You will find that the more you use less familiar ingredients, the more creative and exciting your cooking and eating will become.

The next chapter on salads will, I hope, encourage you to eat more raw fresh food with the hot savoury wholefood dishes you have learnt to cook.

4.

SALADS AND DRESSINGS

Salad days should be every day! A fresh salad eaten daily will definitely help to keep the doctor away but they can, of course, be very boring if all you get is a limp lettuce leaf, a few slices of squashy tomato, peeled soft cucumber perhaps with a bit of grated carrot thrown in. But if you use a variety of fresh fruit and vegetables in the right combination and dress them with a complimentary dressing then they are not only delicious but one of the best aids to a healthy body.

The best way to ensure that you eat a salad daily is to stock the fridge each week with carrots, white or red cabbage, chinese leaf (which is softer than white cabbage and crisper and longer lasting than lettuce), some bean sprouts, mustard and cress, fresh parsley, cucumber, and tomatoes (when not too expensive). Another good tip to encourage more salad eating is to make enough basic salad dressing for several days and store it in a screw-top jar. Then all you have to do is chop a few vegetables, shake the jar and spoon some dressing over your prepared mixture.

I will give you just a few simple salad and dressing recipes but remember, there are endless ways of varying salads using more unusual vegetables and fruits like peppers, raw mushrooms, avocados and courgettes (zucchini), but these are more expensive and you may want to save them for special occasions. For every day, stick to more basic inexpensive vegetables which can become a regular part of your diet.

A very important point to remember with all fresh vegetables and fruit is that when you cut them, valuable vitamin C is gradually destroyed the longer they are exposed to the air. Chop, dress and eat them quickly to ensure that you get most of the nutrients.

I will begin the recipes with dressings as they are vital in making your salads.

Basic Oil and Lemon Dressing
(French Dressing)

This will be enough for one bowl of salad but if you make three times the amount, and store as described above, you will eat more salads because there will be less to prepare.

Imperial (Metric)	American
3 tablespoons corn *or* olive oil	3 tablespoons corn *or* olive oil
I tablespoon fresh lemon juice (about ½ lemon) or I tablespoon cider vinegar	I tablespoon fresh lemon juice (about ½ lemon) or I tablespoon cider vinegar
Good pinch of freshly ground black pepper	Good pinch of freshly ground black pepper
½ teaspoon sea salt	½ teaspoon sea salt
½ teaspoon clear honey	½ teaspoon clear honey
I clove garlic, crushed (optional)	I clove garlic, crushed (optional)
½ level teaspoon dry mustard powder (optional)	½ level teaspoon dry mustard powder (optional)

1 Just shake all the ingredients together in a screw-top jar and spoon over your salad as soon as possible after chopping the vegetables.

Mayonnaise

To make really good mayonnaise quickly and easily you will need a liquidizer. You can buy ready-made mayonnaise, but look at the labels and get one without colouring, flavouring or preservatives in it. Look out for lemon juice and vegetable oil mayonnaise.

Imperial (Metric)	American
I large egg	I large egg
2 tablespoons lemon juice	2 tablespoons lemon juice
I level teaspoon sea salt	I level teaspoon sea salt
½ level teaspoon freshly ground black pepper	½ level teaspoon freshly ground black pepper
½ level teaspoon mustard powder (optional)	½ level teaspoon mustard powder (optional)
⅓ pint (200ml) corn *or* sunflower oil	¾ cup corn *or* sunflower oil

1 Put the egg, lemon juice, salt, pepper, mustard powder and 2 fl oz (60ml/¼ cup) of the oil in the liquidizer.

2 Turn to a low speed and blend well together for 1 minute.

3 Then gradually pour the rest of the oil into the goblet in a steady slow stream, still keeping the speed on low. When thick and creamy, scoop out of the liquidizer into a screw-top jar. Store in the fridge.

Variation — Mayonnaise with Yogurt:

Using the recipe for Mayonnaise all you do is add 1 extra *egg yolk* when putting the whole egg into the goblet. This thickens the mixture. When your mayonnaise is thick scoop it out from the goblet and stir in 2 heaped tablespoons of natural (plain) yogurt.

Now for some tasty and inexpensive salads that are quick to prepare.

Coleslaw
(White Cabbage Salad)

Imperial (Metric)	American
1 lb (455g) of white cabbage, shredded finely	4 cups finely shredded cabbage
2 crisp green eating apples, chopped into small chunks	2 crisp green eating apples, chopped into small chunks
2 oz (50g) raisins	⅓ cup raisins
1 tablespoon onion, very finely chopped (optional)	1 tablespoon onion, very finely chopped (optional)
2 medium carrots, grated	2 medium carrots, grated
6 tablespoons mayonnaise (or more, to taste)	6 tablespoons mayonnaise (or more, to taste)

1 Just mix all the ingredients together and dress with mayonnaise.

Note: Real coleslaw dressing is mayonnaise to which you add a little horseradish root or powder. If using 6 tablespoons mayonnaise just add either 1 teaspoon horseradish powder *or* 1 rounded teaspoon horseradish root.

Chinese Leaf Salad

Once you have eaten Chinese leaf you will search around for more. It is crisp, full of flavour and will last for over a week in the fridge if wrapped in a plastic bag or sealed container. When cutting off the amount you require it is important to slice down the centre lengthwise. The leaves are soft and lettuce-like at the top and crisp and cabbage-like at the base. Your salad should have some of both textures.

Imperial (Metric)	American
4 inches (10cm) cucumber	4 inches cucumber
12 oz (350g) Chinese leaf, sliced thinly	12 ounces Chinese leaf, sliced thinly
1 large carrot, scubbed and grated	1 large carrot, scrubbed and grated
1 punnet mustard and cress	1 punnet mustard and cress
4 firm tomatoes, each cut into 6 segments	4 firm tomatoes, each cut into 6 segments

1 Cut the cucumber into 8 equal slices, then cut each slice into 4 quarters.

2 Mix all ingredients together and dress with several tablespoons of Oil and Lemon French Dressing (see page 64).

Note: This salad will taste delicious with or without the tomatoes.

Shades of Green Salad

This salad is particularly good to serve with hot tomato dishes such as Spaghetti Bolognese or Pizza. Make it just before serving your meal.

Imperial (Metric)	American
½ large Webb's *or* Cos lettuce *or* Chinese leaf	½ large Webb's *or* Cos lettuce *or* Chinese leaf
½ bunch watercress	½ bunch watercress
1 punnet mustard and cress	1 punnet mustard and cress
5 inch (13cm) piece of cucumber, thinly sliced	5 inch piece cucumber, thinly sliced
3 tablespoon fresh chopped parsley	3 tablespoons chopped parsley
4 large spring onions, finely chopped	4 large scallions, finely chopped

1 Wash the ingredients well. Leave to drain in a colander.

2 Chop the lettuce, watercress and mustard and cress coarsely and place in a shallow bowl.

3 Arrange the cucumber slices, slightly overlapping, around the edge as well as in a small circle in the middle.

4 Sprinkle on the chopped parsley and spring onions (scallions).

5 Finally sprinkle on Oil and Lemon French Dressing (page 64).

Tomato, Orange and Cucumber Platter

This is delicious with any rice or millet dish.

Imperial (Metric)	American
4 medium tomatoes	4 medium tomatoes
½ cucumber	½ cucumber
2 medium oranges	2 medium oranges
2 tablespoons chopped chives *or* spring onions	2 tablespoons chives *or* scallions
½ teaspoon basil *or* oregano	½ teaspoon basil *or* oregano

1 Cut the tomatoes and cucumber into thin slices, crosswise. Peel the oranges and do the same.

2 Arrange them, slightly overlapping, in circles in an oval or round shallow serving dish or plate.

3 Sprinkle on the chives or spring onions (scallions) and the basil or oregano.

4 Spoon Oil and Lemon French Dressing (page 64) over this and serve at once.

Potato Salad
(Serves 4)

Imperial (Metric)	American
1½ lbs (700g) potatoes, steamed	1½ pounds potatoes, steamed
4 oz (110g) frozen peas	⅔ cup frozen peas
4 oz (110g) frozen sweetcorn	⅔ cup frozen sweetcorn
2 tender sticks celery	2 tender stalks celery
1 heaped tablespoon onion, very finely chopped	1 heaped tablespoon onion, very finely chopped
3 tablespoons fresh parsley	3 tablespoons fresh parsley
4 tablespoons mayonnaise (page 64), or more if you like	4 tablespoons mayonnaise (page 64), or more if you like

1 Peel the thin skins from the potatoes and cut into small chunks.

2 Cook the peas and sweetcorn for 4 minutes only in a little boiling salted water. Drain them.

3 Chop the celery very finely.

4 Put the potatoes in a serving bowl and stir in the celery, peas, sweetcorn, onion and 2 tablespoons parsley, with a fork.

5 Gently stir in the mayonnaise with a fork.

6 Finally sprinkle the extra finely chopped parsley over the top to garnish.

Note: When choosing the potatoes remember small ones steam quicker. They will be cooked when you can pierce them easily right through with a knitting needle. Don't over cook them. See page 44 on steaming potatoes.

Bean Sprout Salad Delight

Bean sprouts are a very nutritious food. They are high in protein and rich in vitamins, especially B and C. You can buy Chinese bean sprouts cheaply from some supermarkets and greengrocers. These are usually sprouted from little green *mung beans* but you can quite easily sprout your own from a variety of seeds. After one simple recipe I will end this chapter by telling you how to do just that. The recipe for this salad has its own special dressing.

Imperial (Metric)	American
10 oz (275g) bean sprouts	5 cups, bean sprouts
1 carrot, scrubbed and cut into very thin slivers	1 carrot, scrubbed and cut into very thin slivers
2 tablespoons pineapple, chopped (tinned or fresh)	2 tablespoons pineapple, chopped (tinned or fresh)
2 tablespoons green or red pepper, chopped (optional)	2 tablespoons green or red pepper, chopped (optional)
4 large spring onions	4 large scallions

Bean Sprout Salad Dressing:

Imperial (Metric)	American
3 tablespoons corn oil	3 tablespoons corn oil
1 tablespoon lemon juice	1 tablespoon lemon juice
1 teaspoon shoyu	1 teaspoon shoyu
½ teaspoon clear honey	½ teaspoon clear honey
1 clove garlic, crushed	1 clove garlic, crushed

1 Put all the salad ingredients in a bowl.

2 Shake all the ingredients for the bean sprout salad dressing in a screw-top jar and pour it over the salad. Stir well together.

Note: You can use the Oil and Lemon French Dressing (page 64) and the salad will be just as delicious, but it's quite exciting to experiment with different flavours and you might be pleasantly surprised at how good this special dressing is.

How to Grow Your Own Bean Sprouts

You will need a sieve, a large, wide-rimmed clean glass jar, a clean piece of muslin *or* net curtain and an elastic band.

If you have never sprouted seeds before it is best to start with a special packet of sprouting seeds as these are usually selected from fresh dried crops. These can be bought at your local health food or wholefood shop. The quality of the seeds is important when sprouting.

1 Wash 2 tablespoons of seeds well in the sieve and leave them to soak for two hours in cold water.

2 Rinse well in a sieve and then drain all water off.

3 Put them in the glass jar. Cover the jar with the muslin and secure it with the elastic band.

4 Place the jar on its side.

5 Put the jar in a warm place in the kitchen, but not in direct sunlight.

6 Rinse the seeds three times each day by pouring a little warm water in through the muslin then pouring it out, with the muslin still tightly secured.

7 They will take about 3 to 5 days to sprout to the right length, depending on the seeds you use and the room temperature — 60/65°F (15/18°C) is about right.

5.

DESSERTS AND PUDDINGS

Although desserts and puddings are not essential after a main dish it can be a pleasant surprise sometimes to present a treat to round off the meal.

It is, however, important to balance your meals. For instance, if you serve eggs in the main course in the form of an omelette or quiche then you wouldn't choose egg custard tart as a dessert. In the same way, if you have had savoury pies or stuffed baked potatoes then you would be well advised to choose a light sweet such as yogurt whip or fruit jelly, or just fresh fruit salad.

Remember to try and use as little sugar as possible, avoid white flour in your sweet pastries and eat fresh fruit daily.

I will start with the light desserts which can be eaten any day and end with pies, tarts and puddings which I feel should be a treat once or twice a week.

Apricot, Apple and Yogurt Whip
(Serves 6)

You will need a saucepan, a liquidizer, an egg whisk, and 6 individual serving dishes. You can sieve the fruit instead of using a liquidizer.

Imperial (Metric)	American
4 oz (110g) dried apricots, well washed	¾ cup dried apricots, well washed
¾ pint (400ml) apple juice	2 cups apple juice
½ teaspoon cinnamon	½ teaspoon cinnamon
2 large cooking apples, peeled, cored and sliced	2 large cooking apples, peeled, cored and sliced
2 tablespoons clear honey	2 tablespoons clear honey
¼ pint (140ml) natural yogurt	⅔ cup plain yogurt
2 egg whites	2 egg whites
Chopped nuts for decoration	Chopped nuts for decoration

1 Soak the washed apricots in the apple juice and cinnamon overnight.

2 Cook the apricots gently for 10 minutes only.

3 Drain and put the apricots in the liquidizer or into a sieve.

4 Put the apricot juice in the saucepan and add the sliced apple and the honey and cook gently for 10 minutes or until soft.

5 Liquidize the cooked apples with their juice and the apricots until smooth, or sieve the apricots and mix well with the apple mixture. Leave to cool, then stir in the yogurt.

6 Now whisk the egg whites until smooth and fold into the fruit mixture.

7 Spoon into individual dishes and sprinkle with chopped nuts. Chill before serving.

Carob or Chocolate and Mandarin Delight
(Serves 4)

Yogurt cheese is needed to make this so prepare the yogurt as directed the day before you need it, and store in the fridge.

You will need a piece of muslin, a saucepan, a bowl, a mixing bowl, a tablespoon, a cheese grater and 4 individual serving dishes.

Imperial (Metric)	American
½ pint (265ml) natural yogurt	1⅓ cups plain yogurt
4 oz carob *or* chocolate bar	4 ounce carob *or* chocolate bar
¼ pint (140ml) double cream	⅔ cup heavy cream
1 tin unsweetened mandarin oranges	1 can unsweetened mandarin oranges
Flaked almonds for decoration	Slivered almonds for decoration

1 Put the yogurt into a piece of muslin, tie it up and hang it up to drip, to make yogurt cheese. It will take 2 hours at least, but it is best to do this the day before.

2 Melt the carob or chocolate by placing the bar in a bowl over a pan of hot water.

3 Whip the double cream until thick. Stir in yogurt cheese.

4 Stir in the melted chocolate.

5 Drain the mandarins well and and stir gently into the cream and yogurt mixture.

6 Spoon into individual dishes. Sprinkle with almonds. Chill well.

Mandarin and Banana Fluff
(Serves 4)

This is another sweet using mandarins, but is less rich than the previous recipe. You will need 4 individual serving dishes, a bowl, a saucepan, an egg whisk and a small wooden spoon.

Imperial (Metric)	American
2 small oranges	2 small oranges
2 eggs, separated	2 eggs, separated
I teaspoon honey	I teaspoon honey
2 small bananas	2 small bananas
2 teaspoons lemon juice	2 teaspoons lemon juice
I small tin mandarins, well drained	I small can mandarins, well drained

1 Heat some water in the saucepan and place the bowl over it.

2 Wash the oranges, wipe and grate the peel. Squeeze the juice.

3 Mix egg yolks, orange rind and juice, and honey, then put them in the bowl over the hot water. Cook, stirring all the time, until the mixture thickens. Leave to cool.

4 Mash the bananas with the lemon juice.

5 Fold the bananas into the cooled egg yolk mixture.

6 Whisk egg whites until stiff. Fold into the yolk mixture with the mandarins.

7 Spoon into serving dishes and chill.

Carob Mousse

This is a rich sweet for special occasions. You will need a saucepan, half full of hot water, a bowl to melt the carob bar in, a metal spoon, an egg whisk, a cheese grater and 6 individual serving dishes.

Imperial (Metric)	American
8 oz (225g) carob bar	8 ounce carob bar
4 eggs, separated	4 eggs, separated
Rind of 1 small orange, finely grated	Rind of 1 small orange, finely grated
1 tablespoon orange juice	1 tablespoon orange juice
2 tablespoons natural yogurt	2 tablespoons plain yogurt

1 Melt the carob bar in the bowl over hot water.

2 Take off the heat and add the egg yolks, with the orange rind and juice. Leave to cool.

3 Stir in the yogurt.

4 Whisk the egg whites until stiff.

5 Lightly fold this into the carob mixture with the metal spoon. Do not mix too hard.

6 Spoon into individual serving dishes and chill for at least 2 hour before serving.

Fruit Jelly

I use *Gelozone* instead of gelatine to make jellies. *Gelozone* is a dried and powdered seaweed called carrageen. Gelatine is prepared from the bones and hides of animals. There are various recipe suggestions on the *Gelozone* packets which show that it can be used instead of gelatine in most recipes. You will need a saucepan, a wooden spoon and a jelly mould or 4 individual serving dishes.

Imperial (Metric)	American
I pint (575ml) apple juice	2½ cups apple juice
2 bananas, sliced into rounds	2 bananas, sliced into rounds
Either 2 good slices of fresh pineapple chopped into triangles *or* I small tin pineapple, well drained	Either 2 good slices of fresh pineapple chopped into triangles *or* I small can pineapple, well drained
2 rounded teaspoons *Gelozone*	2 rounded teaspoons *Gelozone*
A little honey	A little honey

1 Mix the *Gelozone* with a little of the cold apple juice.

2 Put in the saucepan and slowly add the rest of the apple juice.

3 Bring to the boil stirring continuously. Simmer for 2 minutes.

4 Stir in a little honey if not sweet enough.

5 Arrange the fruit in the bottom of the mould, alternating banana rounds and pineapple triangles to form a pattern.

6 Pour in the liquid jelly. Leave it to cool and then set in the fridge. *Gelozone* sets quicker than gelatine.

Note: If the jelly does not turn out of the mould easily, just immerse it (not quite up to the rim) in hot water for 30 seconds then turn out onto a serving dish.

Ice-Cream
(Serves 4 to 6)

Making your own ice-cream is not only very simple but can provide you with a delicious and nutritious dessert. Many commercial ice-creams have added colouring and flavourings and rarely contain natural ingredients.

I will give you just a few recipes to try out but the varieties you can make are endless.

Basic Vanilla Ice-Cream

You will need a mixing bowl, an egg whisk and a freezer container.

Imperial (Metric)	American
2 large eggs	2 large eggs
2 oz (50g) light raw cane *soft* sugar *or 2* tablespoons honey	⅓ cup light raw cane *soft* sugar *or 2* tablespoons honey
¼ pint (140ml) double cream with ¼ pint (140ml) single cream *or* ½ pint (275ml) evaporated milk	⅔ cup heavy cream with ⅔ cup light cream *or* 1⅓ cups evaporated milk
½ teaspoon natural vanilla essence	½ teaspoon natural vanilla essence

1 Put the eggs and sugar into a bowl. Whisk until thick and creamy.

2 If using cream, whisk the double (heavy) cream until it is firm but not stiff. Then gradually whisk in the single light cream. If using evaporated milk whisk until stiff.

3 Add the vanilla essence.

4 Fold this mixture into the beaten eggs and sugar.

5 Spoon into a freezer container and freeze until firm.

Variations:
The addition of 2 oz (50g/½ cup) chopped toasted hazelnuts will give a lovely flavour to your basic ice-cream.

Fruit Ice-Cream

All you do to make fabulous fruit ice-cream is add *1 cup* of fruit purée to the basic ice-cream recipe. Leave out the vanilla and add the fruit at stage 3 in the recipe.

The best fruits are washed and sieved fresh strawberries, raspberries or cooked, sieved and cooled fresh or dried apricots. Make sure the fruit purée is thick not watery.

Custard Flan
(Makes 6 good-sized portions)

Custard flans or tarts can be either absolutely delicious or a wobbly soggy mess. The secret is to have a light, crisp pastry base and a firm custard filling.

I have experimented with this much-loved sweet and found that using eggs and egg yolks achieves the best results. This means that you will have egg whites left over but these need not be wasted. They can always be used up in an Apricot, Apple and Yogurt Whip (page 72).

This recipe is for a large flan. It is still delicious the day after it is made. When making sweet pastry I sometimes use 85 per cent extraction flour as this achieves a lighter mixture appropriate for sweet dishes. This pastry is great for apple pie or any other sweet pastry recipe.

You will need a mixing bowl, a wooden spoon, a 10 inch (25cm) flan case or sandwich tin, a medium-sized saucepan, an egg whisk, a sieve, a palette knife and a plastic bag.

For the Sweet Pastry:

Imperial (Metric)	American
4 oz (100g) polyunsaturated margarine	½ cup polyunsaturated margarine
I rounded dessertspoon soft dark raw cane sugar	2 rounded teaspoons soft dark raw cane sugar
Pinch of sea salt	Pinch of sea salt
8 oz (225g) 85 per cent wholemeal flour	2 cups 85 per cent wholewheat flour
3 tablespoons cold water	3 tablespoons cold water
I tablespoon bran	I tablespoon bran

1 Set the oven at 400°F/200°C (Gas Mark 6).

2 Cream the polyunsaturated margarine and sugar in the mixing bowl for 1 minute only.

3 Mix the sea salt into the flour.

4 Add the water to the polyunsaturated margarine and sugar cream, plus 2 tablespoons of the flour.

5 Cream together and gradually add the rest of the flour, using your hands as you add the last few spoonfuls.

6 Knead the dough for 2 minutes. Flatten it. Put it into a plastic bag and either place in the fridge for 30 minutes or in the freezer for 7 minutes.

7 Sprinkle the bran on the work-top, put the pastry on top, sprinkle a little bran on the pastry and cover with the plastic bag. Roll out over the plastic. This makes it easy to roll it out thinly without adding extra flour. Slide a palette knife under the pastry, curl it round your rolling-pin and lift into the flan case. Press to fit and trim the edges.

8 Prick the base and bake for 10 minutes in the centre of the oven.

For the Custard Filling:

Imperial (Metric)	American
¾ pint (425ml) milk	2 cups milk
I vanilla pod *or* a few drop of natural vanilla essence	I vanilla pod or a few drops of natural vanilla essence
2 eggs	2 eggs
2 egg yolks	2 egg yolks
I generous tablespoon Demerara sugar	I generous tablespoon Demerara sugar
Little freshly grated nutmeg for the top.	Little freshly grated nutmeg for the top

1 Set oven between 325°F and 350°F/160°C and 180°C (Gas Mark 3 and 4).

2 Heat the milk with the vanilla pod or vanilla essence. Do not boil, just warm.

3 Beat eggs with the sugar, in a bowl, for 1 minute.

4 Remove the vanilla pod, if used (rinse and dry it to use again). Pour the warm milk over the beaten eggs.

5 Now strain the egg and milk mixture into the hot pastry case.

6 Grate a little fresh nutmeg over this.

7 Bake in the centre of the oven for 35 to 40 minutes until the custard has set. Cool before cutting.

Semolina Pudding
(Serves 3)

This is a very simple pudding that can be eaten at breakfast time or after a light lunch or supper. Choose wholewheat semolina, which can be obtained from wholefood or health food stores.

You will need a medium-sized thick saucepan, a wooden spoon and 3 individual bowls.

Imperial (Metric)	American
1 pint (575ml) milk	2½ cups milk
Good pinch of freshly grated nutmeg	Good pinch of freshly grated nutmeg
2 oz (50g) wholewheat semolina	½ cup wholewheat semolina
1 tablespoon ground almonds (optional)	1 tablespoon ground almonds (optional)
1 dessertspoon clear honey	2 teaspoons clear honey
2 tablespoons apple juice concentrate	2 tablespoons apple juice concentrate

1 Put the milk and nutmeg in the saucepan. Bring to the boil.

2 Add the semolina, ground almonds (if used) and honey, stirring in quickly.

3 Stir until the mixture thickens (this takes just 1 minute).

4 Cook gently on very low heat for 3 minutes.

5 To serve, put into individual bowls and trickle a little apple juice concentrate over the top.

Apple and Apricot Tart

This recipe makes a change from apple pie and is delicious hot or cold. You will need a saucepan and 1 batch of Sweet Pastry (page 78). Follow the instructions for making the pastry but, when rolling out, save some of the pastry dough for a little lattice-work pattern on top of the fruit.

Bake the pastry case at 400°F/200°C (Gas Mark 6) for 10 minutes. You will need a bowl, a sieve and a saucepan.

For the Filling:

Imperial (Metric)	American
4 oz (110g) dried apricot pieces, washed and soaked in ¾ pint (425ml) cold water with 1 tablespoon honey	⅔ cup dried apricots pieces, washed and soaked in 2 cups cold water with 1 tablespoon honey
2 large cooking apples, thinly peeled and sliced	2 large cooking apples, thinly peeled and sliced
2 tablespoons apple juice concentrate	2 tablespoons apple juice concentrate
½ teaspoon ground cinnamon	½ teaspoon ground cinnamon
¼ teaspoon clove powder (optional)	¼ teaspoon clove powder (optional)
2 teaspoons Barbados sugar or honey (optional)	2 teaspoons Barbados sugar or honey (optional)

1 Set the oven at 350°F/180°C (Gas Mark 4).

2 Cook the soaked apricots for 10 minutes, then drain in a sieve, reserving the juice.

3 Put the juice back into the saucepan and cook the apples in this, with the apple juice concentrate and spices, until soft. Add a few drops of extra water if necessary.

4 Press the apricots through the sieve or liquidize to a purée.

5 Mix half the apricot purée with the cooked apples and spread the mixture over the cooked pastry case.

6 Now taste the other half of the apricot purée and, if it is not sweet enough for your taste, add Barbados sugar or honey. Mix well in and spread this over the apple and apricot mixture.

7 Roll out the remaining pastry into long thin strips. Make a criss-cross lattice pattern on top of the filling. Bake for 15 to 20 minutes until the lattice strips are lightly browned.

Fruit Crumble

This is the easiest hot pudding of all. You will need an 8 inch (20cm) pudding dish at least 3 inches (7.5cm) deep, a mixing bowl and cool hands. Set the oven at 375°F/190°C (Gas Mark 5).

For the Crumble Topping:

Imperial (Metric)	American
6 oz (175g) wholemeal flour	1½ cups wholewheat flour
Pinch of sea salt	Pinch of sea salt
3 oz (75g) polyunsaturated margarine, very cold	⅓ cup polyunsaturated margarine, very cold
2 level tablespoons Barbados sugar	2 level tablespoons Barbados sugar
2 tablespoons sesame seeds or chopped sunflower seeds	2 tablespoons sesame seeds, or chopped sunflower seeds

1 Put the flour and salt into the bowl. Rub in the margarine to form a breadcrumb-like mixture.

2 Add the sugar and seeds and rub in thoroughly.

Fruit Filling I:

Imperial (Metric)	American
1½ lb (680g) cooking apples	1½ pounds cooking apples
½ teaspoon cinnamon	½ teaspoon cinnamon
¼ teaspoon clove powder or 4 cloves	¼ teaspoon clove powder or 4 cloves
4 tablespoons apple juice concentrate and 1 tablespoon honey or 3 tablespoons Barbados sugar	4 tablespoons apple juice concentrate and 1 tablespoon honey or 3 tablespoons Barbados sugar

1 Thinly peel the apples, core and thinly slice. Arrange in the bottom of the pudding dish.

2 Stir in the spices and pour over the apple juice and honey. Fork it in gently.

3 Sprinkle the crumble mixture on top.

4 Bake in the centre of the oven for 40 minutes. If top is getting too brown, place a piece of greaseproof (wax) paper over the top, as the fruit will need 40 minutes to cook.

Fruit Filling II:

Imperial (Metric)	American
1¼ lb (725g) cooking apples	1¼ pounds cooking apples
8 oz (225g) fresh blackberries	2 cups fresh blackberries
2 oz (50g) Barbados sugar *or* 2 tablespoons clear honey	⅓ cup Barbados sugar *or* 2 tablespoons clear honey
2 tablespoons cold water	2 tablespoons cold water

1 Thinly peel, core and thinly slice the apples.

2 Place all the ingredients in the baking dish.

3 Toss gently with a fork to ensure the sweetner is evenly distributed.

4 Sprinkle the crumble over the top and proceed as for Filling I.

Filling III:

Imperial (Metric)	American
3 large cooking apples	3 large cooking apples
3 tablespoons water	3 tablespoons water
1 tablespoon honey	1 tablespoon honey
1 level teaspoon cinnamon	1 level teaspoon cinnamon
4 oz (110g) stoned dates	¾ cup pitted dates

1 Peel, core and thinly slice the apples.

2 In a saucepan, heat the water, honey, cinnamon and dates on low heat. Mix to a smooth purée.

3 Place one layer of apples into the baking dish. Spread over some of the date purée.

4 Repeat, finishing with a layer of date mixture.

5 Cover with crumble mixture and bake as for Filling I.

Note: You can add soaked uncooked apricots or any fruit you like, just make it up to 2 pounds (900g) in weight. Remember, when using dried fruit such as apricots, that the weight you take into account is that after they have been soaked. Four ounces (100g) dried apricots will usually weigh 12 ounces (375g) when soaked.

6.

TEA-TIME

In this chapter I include some old favourites which I think you will find taste even better using more healthy ingredients.

Most shop-bought cakes and biscuits contain too much sugar, saturated animal fat and little or no fibre because white flour is used. As I have already mentioned in the Introduction (page 8), we need fibre to get rid of waste products from our bodies. Mass-produced cakes and biscuits also contain artificial colourings, flavourings and preservatives which can be harmful to our health.

It's much better to make your own tea-time treats and jam pack them with as much goodness as possible. Light and delicious cakes and munchy melt-in-the-mouth biscuits can all be achieved using wholemeal flour and other wholesome ingredients.

No tea-time is complete without a tasty loaf of bread, so the recipes begin with a wholemeal bread dough which will not only make beautiful bread, but can be used as a pizza base and for making pitta bread. If you have never eaten stuffed pitta bread, which is a Middle Eastern and Greek flat bread, then this is a good wholemeal beginning. In these countries the pitta is cut diagonally, each half is then slit open to form a pocket which is filled with salad and a purée of chick peas called Hummous. In the recipe I will show you another way of preparing pitta.

Breads

When making a bread dough — which does take time — I never see the point in just ending up with one or two loaves of bread which disappear into hungry mouths as soon as they descend onto the cooling rack.

With just 1½ pounds (750g) of strong wholemeal flour you can make one loaf of bread and six pitta breads, or one loaf of bread and a pizza base. Strong flour has more gluten which means more protein and which helps the dough to rise better. The sesame seeds in the recipe are not essential but add a delicious flavour and more important they contain valuable minerals and vitamins. I use bran for rolling out the pittas and pizza bread because this does not dry the dough and gives a nice texture when cooked.

Basic Wholemeal Sesame Bread and Pitta Dough

You will need a mixing bowl, 2 measuring jugs, a rolling pin, an oiled and floured bread tin (1 pound/500g size), 2 baking trays oiled and sprinkled with bran, and 4 large oiled plastic bags (big enough to slide your baking trays into).

Imperial (Metric)	American
1½ lb strong wholemeal flour	6 cups wholewheat flour
1 level dessertspoon sea salt	2 level teaspoons sea salt
2 rounded tablespoons sesame seeds	2 rounded tablespoons sesame seeds
1 level tablespoon dried yeast (approx ¾ oz /15g)	1 level tablespoon dried yeast
¾ pint (400ml) warm water	2 cups warm water
1 dessertspoon malt extract	2 teaspoons malt extract
1 level teaspoon Barbados sugar	1 level teaspoon Barbados sugar
1 tablespoon corn or sunflower oil, water or beaten egg to glaze	1 tablespoon corn or sunflower oil, water or beaten egg to glaze
Extra sesame seeds for top of loaf	Extra sesame seeds for top of loaf

1 Put the flour, sea salt and first amount of sesame seeds into a bowl. Mix well together.

2 Measure ⅓ pint (200ml/¾ cup) warm water in one jug. Sprinkle on the dried yeast and the sugar. Stir well, cover with a cloth and leave to froth in a warm place — not a hot surface or the yeast will die — for 5 to 7 minutes.

3 In another jug, measure out ⅓ pint (200ml)/¾ cup warm water. Stir in the malt extract and the corn oil. Mix well together.

4 When the yeast liquid has frothed, make a well in the centre of the flour mixture and pour both jugs of liquid into the centre. Form all this into a soft dough.

5 Knead for 7 minutes on a lightly floured formica top. (Do not knead on an unsealed wooden table or the dough will stick and you will probably have to add extra flour which will dry out your dough.)

6 Put the dough into an oiled plastic bag. Press out the air and tie the opening. Put into a towel and leave to rise in a warm but not hot place for 40 minutes or until double in size. Your dough is now ready.

To make one loaf of bread:

1 Take dough out of plastic bag and knead for 2 minutes only. Cut off 1½ pounds (700g) which will leave you with about 1 pound (450g) which you should return to the plastic bag and reserve to use for pitta breads or pizza.

2 Roll out the dough to an oval shape the length of your bread tin. Now roll it over into a Swiss-roll shape.

3 Put this into the tin and press it gently down to cover the whole of the bottom.

4 Cover the tin with an oiled plastic bag and leave to rise in a warm place until double in size (about 30 minutes). While it is rising, heat the oven on to 450°F/230°C (Gas Mark 8).

5 When bread is well risen, brush the top lightly with warm water or egg and sprinkle on some sesame seeds.

6 Place in the centre of the oven and bake for 10 minutes, then turn oven down to 350°F/180°C (Gas Mark 4) and continue baking for 25 minutes more.

7 Remove the tin from the oven and cool for 2 minutes. Slide a palette knife all around the edges and turn bread out onto a cooling rack.

To make 6 Pitta Breads:

1 While your bread is rising in the tin start to roll out the pittas.

2 Take out the remaining dough. Knead it for 1 minute. Form into a sausage shape and cut into 6 even-sized pieces.

3 Put 5 pieces back into the bag. Sprinkle some bran onto a smooth surface and roll out each piece of dough in turn to a thin oval shape approx. 8 inches (20cm) long and 4 inches (10cm) wide.

4 Place three on each baking tray and slide the trays into plastic bags.

5 Let them rise for approx. 20 minutes until lightly swelling. They do not rise very much so don't wait too long.

6 Set oven to 450°F/230°C (Gas Mark 8). Bake the pittas, one tray at a time, for 5 minutes only. They will puff up either completely into an oval balloon or puff up in parts. Either way they will still be good pitta breads. Do not overcook; 5 minutes really is long enough. Slide a palette knife under each pitta and cool on a wire rack.

Note: To serve, slice open the pittas and put grated cheese on one side. Grill until it bubbles. Put a little margarine on the other side. Put salad such as beansprouts, cucumber, tomato, Chinese leaf etc., on top of the cheese. Top with other half of the pitta and grill to warm the top only.

You can also fill this with vegetable pâté and salad or any other sandwich filling of your choice. Delicious hot or cold.

Pizza
(6 portions)

You will need 1 round pizza tray, oiled and sprinkled with bran. The tray can be an 11 inch (27cm) diameter round or a 12 × 9 inch (30 × 23cm) rectangle. You will also need a medium-sized, thick saucepan and wooden spoon for the topping.

1 Sprinkle some bran on a smooth, clean surface.

2 Roll the dough into a round or rectangle shape roughly the size of your tin.

3 Spread the dough, pressing gently, to the extreme edge of your tin.

4 Slide the tin into an oiled plastic bag and leave to rise for 20 to 30 minutes, whilst preparing the topping.

Pizza Sauce:

Imperial (Metric)	American
I medium onion, chopped	I medium onion, chopped
I clove garlic, crushed	I clove garlic, crushed
2 sticks celery, finely chopped	2 stalks celery, finely chopped
2 tablespoons corn *or* sunflower oil	2 tablespoons corn *or* sunflower oil
I small green pepper, chopped	I small green pepper, chopped
2 oz (50g) button mushrooms, sliced (optional)	I cup button mushrooms, sliced (optional)
I teaspoon basil	I teaspoon basil
I bay leaf	I bay leaf
14-oz (400g) tin tomatoes	14 ounces canned tomatoes
I tablespoon tomato purée	I tablespoon tomato paste
Sea salt and freshly ground black pepper to taste	Sea salt and freshly ground black pepper to taste
6 oz (175g) grated Cheddar cheese	1½ cups grated Cheddar cheese
I oz (25g) pumpkin seeds (sunflower seeds can be used instead)	2 tablespoons pumpkin seeds (sunflower seeds can be used instead)
I level teaspoon oregano	I level teaspoon oregano

1 Sauté the onion, garlic and celery in the oil for 5 minutes.

2 Add the peppers and mushrooms (if you are including mushrooms) and fry for 3 more minutes. Stir in the basil and bay leaf.

3 Now drain off ½ cup of tomato juice from your can of tomatoes and put the juice in the fridge. You can use this for soups or sauces another day.

4 Chop the tomatoes and add these, with the tomato purée (paste), to the cooking vegetables.

5 Stir all well together and add a little sea salt and freshly ground black pepper to your own taste.

6 Simmer the sauce with the lid on for 20 minutes only. By this time your pizza dough should be puffed up ready for the sauce.

7 Spoon the hot sauce on top of the risen dough. Leave 1 inch (2.5cm) of dough uncovered all around the edge.

8 Sprinkle the grated cheese over the sauce. Then sprinkle on the pumpkin seeds (sunflower seeds could be used instead) and oregano.

9 Bake in the middle of the oven at 400°F/200°C (Gas Mark 6) for 30 minutes. Leave to set for 10 minutes before cutting. Serve with a salad which has no tomatoes in it.

Granary French Loaf
(Makes 2)

You will need a mixing bowl, a measuring jug, a fork, a rolling pin, one large baking tray, and a large oiled, polythene bag (big enough to slide your baking tray into).

Imperial (Metric)	American
I lb (455g) granary flour	4 cups granary flour
8 oz (225g) 100% strong wholemeal flour	2 cups 100% strong wholewheat flour
I teaspoon sea salt	I teaspoon sea salt
¾ pint (450ml) warm water	2 cups warm water
I level teaspoon Barbados sugar	I level teaspoon Barbados sugar
½ oz (15g) dried yeast	2 level teaspoons dried yeast
I small egg	I small egg
I tablespoon sunflower oil	I tablespoon sunflower oil
I level tablespoon sesame seeds for top of loaves	I level tablespoon sesame seeds for top of loaves

1 Put flour and salt in a mixing bowl.

2 Measure water in the jug (it should just feel warm to your fingertips), sprinkle in the sugar and dried yeast. Stir briskly with a fork and leave to froth in a warm (not hot) place for 10 minutes.

3 Beat egg and oil with a fork.

4 When yeast liquid is frothy, make a well in the middle of the flour and pour it in with the egg and oil.

5 Blend ingredients together to form a soft dough.

6 Knead for 10 minutes. Flour your hands if the dough sticks a bit. Do not use too much flour on the work surface.

7 Place the dough in the oiled polythene bag. Press out the air and tie the opening.

8 Leave to rise in a warm place until double in size — about 45 minutes to 1 hour.

9 Take out dough and knead for 2 minutes only. Break into two equal portions. Put one back in the bag while you form the other into a loaf shape.

10 To do this, roll dough out with the rolling pin to an oval shape 10 inches (25cm) long and 7 inches (17.5cm) wide. Curl the dough over like a Swiss roll, lengthwise, pressing gently together to form a french loaf shape about 12 inches (30cm) long. Place this on the oiled baking tray.

11 Repeat this with the other half of the dough.

12 Slide the baking tray into the polythene bag, making sure that there is enough space for the loaves to double in size. While rising, set oven to 425°F/220°C (Gas Mark 7).

13. Leave to rise in a warm place for about 30 minutes.

14 When risen, make 5 slanting slits with the back of a knife on the top of the loaves. Brush with a little warm water and sprinkle on the sesame seeds.

15 Bake in the preheated oven on the shelf just above the centre for 15 minutes. Then turn the loaves upside down and bake for 3 minutes more.

16 Cool on a wire rack.

Hot Cross Buns or Easter Loaf

I make this tasty Russian loaf mixture into Hot Cross Buns at Easter time. They are much more delicious than shop bought buns and far healthier. You will need 2 well-greased baking trays, a mixing bowl, a measuring jug, a wooden spoon, a cheese grater and two plastic bags to slide trays into.

Imperial (Metric)	American
I oz (28g) fresh yeast	2½ tablespoons fresh yeast
I oz (25g) Barbados sugar	2 tablespoons Barbados sugar
½ pint (275ml) warm (not hot) milk	1⅓ cups warm (not hot) milk
2 large egg yolks	2 large egg yolks
Coarsely grated rind of I small orange	Coarsely grated rind of I small orange
Coarsely grated rind of I lemon	Coarsely grated rind of I lemon
I lb (450g) wholemeal flour	4 cups wholewheat flour
2 oz polyunsaturated margarine, melted	¼ cup polyunsaturated margarine, melted
5 oz dried fruit (sultanas, raisins mixed)	¾ cup dried fruit (mixed raisins)

1 Cream the yeast, 1 teaspoon of the sugar and a little of the milk until smooth. Add the rest of the milk and leave to froth for 10 minutes in a warm place.

2 Put the egg yolks in the mixing bowl, stir in the orange and lemon peel, sugar and the frothy yeast mixture.

3 Gradually stir in 8 oz (225g/2 cups) of the flour.

4 Trickle in the melted but *not hot* margarine, stirring as you trickle.

5 Now mix the dried fruit with the rest of the flour.

6 Gradually add this, little by little, to the mixture. You will have to mould the dough with your hands as you near the end of adding the fruit and flour.

7 The dough will be a bit sticky, but turn it out onto a lightly floured surface. Flour your hands and knead for 7 minutes. During kneading, flour your hands again as necessary. Do not add flour to the dough.

8 Put the dough into an oiled plastic bag and leave to rise in a warm place for 40 minutes until the dough has doubled in size.

9 Turn out the dough, flour your hands and knead for 2 minutes.

10 Divide into 12 equal pieces (each will weigh just under 3 ounces/75g) and put the pieces back into the bag, taking them out one by one as you roll them into balls.

11 Place 6 balls on each baking tray.

12 Slide the trays into the oiled plastic bags and leave to rise in a warm place for 30 minutes or until doubled in size. Heat the oven to 400°F/200°C (Gas Mark 6).

13 When well risen make a very light indent on the top of each with the back of a knife, in the shape of a cross.

14 To bake, place one tray just above centre of the oven and one tray just under centre. Change the trays around after 7 minutes and continue to bake for another 7-10 minutes.

15 To give that shiny top which hot cross buns have, just mix 2 teaspoons hot water with 2 teaspoons of Barbados sugar and brush the top of the buns as soon as they are removed from the oven. Cool on a wire rack.

Russian Easter Loaf

You will need a 2 pounds (1 kilo) loaf tin, well greased. Use exactly the same recipe as for Hot Cross Buns but form the risen dough into a loaf shape and, using your knuckles, press it gently into the loaf tin. Slide the tin into an oiled plastic bag and let it rise until doubled in size. Bake in centre of the oven for 15 minutes at 400°F/200°C (Gas Mark 6). Then turn down the heat to 375°F/190°C (Gas Mark 5) and bake for 25 minutes more.

Malt and Honey Loaf

This loaf is delicious, moist and lovely sliced and spread with polyunsaturated margarine or butter for tea-time. It is quick and easy to make.

You will need a 1 lb (450g/6 cups) loaf tin, greased and lined, a medium-sized saucepan, a wooden spoon, a small bowl for beating the egg and a fork.

Imperial (Metric)	American
2 level tablespoons honey	2 level tablespoons honey
3 level tablespoons malt extract	3 level tablespoons malt extract
3½ fl oz (75ml) water	½ cup water
6 oz (175g) wholemeal flour	1½ cups wholewheat flour
2 oz (50g) raisins or sultanas	⅓ cup dark or golden seedless raisins
1 heaped teaspoon baking powder	1 heaped teaspoon baking powder
1 large egg	1 large egg

1 Set oven at 375°F/190°C (Gas Mark 5).

2 Warm together the honey, malt and water in a saucepan. Do not overheat.

3 Add the dry ingredients.

4 Beat egg then stir this into the mixture.

5 Pour into the greased and lined tin. Bake in centre of the oven for 45 minutes to 1 hour.

Carrot Cake

You can use oil instead of margarine in many cake recipes. It's easy to mix and produces a light-textured cake. You will need a 1 lb (450g/6 cup) loaf tin or a 7 inch (18cm) round cake tin, greased and lined, a cheese grater, an egg whisk, a mixing bowl, a wooden spoon and two small bowls.

Imperial (Metric)	American
6 fl oz (175ml) corn oil *or* sunflower oil	¾ cup corn oil *or* sunflower oil
4 oz (110g) Barbados sugar	⅔ cup Barbados sugar
½ level teaspoon clove powder	½ level teaspoon clove powder
Good pinch of sea salt	Good pinch of sea salt
2 large eggs, separated	2 large eggs, separated
6 oz self-raising/wholemeal flour	1½ cups of self-raising wholewheat flour
2 oz (50g) chopped hazelnuts *or* chopped sunflower seeds	½ cup chopped filberts *or* chopped sunflower seeds
8 oz (225g) finely grated carrot	1½ cups finely grated carrot

1 Set the oven at 325°F/170°C (Gas Mark 3).

2 Beat the oil and sugar together for 1 minute.

3 Add the clove powder and sea salt. Stir well in.

4 Whisk the egg whites for 30 seconds. Whisk the yolks for 30 seconds.

5 Add the whites to the oil and sugar. Stir in.

6 Add the yolks and fold well in.

7 Add the flour, folding in lightly.

8 Add the chopped nuts.

9 Finally, stir in the grated carrot. Put the mixture into the baking tin and bake for 1¼ hours in the centre of the oven.

Eggless and Sugarless Tutti Frutti Cake

This is a very easy boil-in-the-pot cake. You will need a medium-sized thick saucepan, a wooden spoon, a mixing bowl and an 8 inch (20cm) round loose-bottomed tin, greased and lined.

Imperial (Metric)	American
6 fl oz (175ml) clear honey	½ cup clear honey
3 oz (75g) carrot, finely grated	⅔ cup carrot, finely grated
2 oz (50g) sultanas or raisins	⅓ cup dark or golden seedless raisins
2 oz (50g) chopped dates	⅓ cup chopped dates
4 oz (110g) polyunsaturated margarine	½ cup polyunsaturated margarine
I level teaspoon cinnamon	I level teaspoon cinnamon
¼ teaspoon clove powder	¼ teaspoon clove powder
¼ teaspon ground nutmeg	¼ teaspoon ground nutmeg
6 fl oz (175ml) water	¾ cup water
6 oz (175g) wholemeal flour	1½ cups wholewheat flour
2 level teaspoons bicarbonate of soda	2 level teaspoons baking soda
2 oz (50g) hazelnuts, chopped	½ cup chopped filberts

1 Set the oven at 350°F/180°C (Gas Mark 4).

2 Put the honey, carrots, raisins, dates, margarine, cinnamon, clove powder, nutmeg and water in a saucepan.

3 Bring to the boil then turn the heat down. Simmer for 5 minutes, uncovered. Cool for 15 minutes.

4 Mix the flour, bicarbonate of soda (baking soda) and nuts in a bowl. When the liquid mixture has cooled stir the flour mixture into the saucepan, and gently mix thoroughly.

5 Put the mixture into the tin and bake in the centre of the oven for 1 hour.

Coconut and Orange Cake

You will need a 7 inch (18cm) round cake tin, greased and lined, a cheese grater, a mixing bowl, a wooden spoon, an egg whisk and 2 small bowls in which to separate the eggs.

Imperial (Metric)	American
6 oz (175g) polyunsaturated margarine	¾ cup polyunsaturated margarine
6 oz (175g) soft raw cane sugar	I cup soft raw cane sugar
3 eggs, separated	3 eggs, separated
6 oz self-raising wholemeal flour	1½ cups self-raising wholewheat flour
4 oz (110g) desiccated coconut	1⅓ cups desiccated coconut
Juice and rind of I medium orange	Juice and rind of I medium orange

1 Set the oven at 375°F/190°C (Gas Mark 5).

2 Cream the margarine and sugar for 3 minutes only. The mixture *does not* have to be light and fluffy.

3 Beat the egg whites for 30 seconds.

4 Beat the egg yolks for 30 seconds.

5 Add the whites, folding in gently.

6 Add the yolks, folding in gently.

7 Fold in the flour and coconut.

8 Finally, add the juice and the rind of the orange and put the mixture into the baking tin.

9 Bake in the centre of the oven for 45 minutes.

Coconut and Orange Buns
(Makes 18)

This recipe is similar to the Coconut and Orange Cake recipe above but is made lighter by mixing the margarine and sugar until it is light and fluffy and adding the beaten eggs a spoonful at a time.

You will need 18 paper bun cases in patty tins, a mixing bowl, a wooden spoon, a small bowl in which to whisk eggs, an egg whisk, a cheese grater and a teaspoon.

Imperial (Metric)	American
4 oz (110g) polyunsaturated margarine	½ cup polyunsaturated margarine
4 oz (110g) soft dark raw cane sugar	⅔ cup soft dark raw cane sugar
2 large eggs	2 large eggs
4 oz (110g) self-raising wholemeal flour	1 cup self-raising wholewheat flour
3 oz (75g) desiccated coconut	1 cup dessicated coconut
Juice and rind of ½ medium orange	Juice and rind of ½ medium orange

1 Set the oven at 375°F/190°C (Gas Mark 5).

2 Cream the margarine and sugar for 5 to 7 minutes until light and fluffy.

3 Beat the eggs for 1 minute.

4 Add the egg mixture 1 spoonful at a time, folding in each spoonful before adding the next.

5 Just before the final spoonful, add 1 tablespoon of the flour.

6 Now fold in the flour gradually tablespoon by tablespoon.

7 Add the coconut still folding in gently.

8 Finally stir in the juice and rind. Using a teaspoon divide the mixture evenly into the paper cake cases. Bake for 15-20 minutes only.

Apple Cake

This cake is delicious hot with custard sauce or natural yogurt for a dessert or cold, sliced, for tea-time.

You will need a 7 inch (18cm) round cake tin or a 1 lb (450g/6 cup) loaf tin, a mixing bowl, a wooden spoon, a sharp knife, a potato peeler and a small bowl for the eggs. Leave the skins on the apples, as they soften while the cake is baking.

Imperial (Metric)	American
6 oz (175g) self-raising wholemeal flour	1½ cups self-raising wholewheat flour
¼ teaspoon clove powder	¼ teaspoon clove powder
½ level teaspoon cinnamon	½ level teaspoon cinnamon
4 oz (110g) polyunsaturated margarine, chilled	½ cup polyunsaturated margarine, chilled
4 oz (110g) Barbados sugar	⅔ cup Barbados sugar
3 oz (75g) sultanas	½ cup golden seedless raisins
8 oz (225g) cooking apples, washed, cored and chopped into ½ inch (1cm) pieces	2½ cups cooking apples, washed, cored and chopped into ½ inch pieces
2 large eggs, beaten	2 large eggs, beaten

1 Set the oven at 350°F/180°C (Gas Mark 4).

2 Put the flour and spices in a bowl and mix together.

3 Rub in the margarine until mixture looks like rough breadcrumbs.

4 Add the sugar and sultanas (golden seedless raisins).

5 Stir the apples into mixture. Add the beaten eggs. The mixture will seem a little stiff but it will become more moist as the apples cook.

6 Put the mixture into the tin and bake for 1¼ hours.

Carob Birthday Cake

Carob powder or flour is made from the bean of the locust tree. It tastes very much like chocolate but unlike chocolate it does not contain caffeine or oxalic acid, both of which can be harmful to your health. The powder is much cheaper than cocoa and is naturally sweet.

In the Bible story about St. John the Baptist we are told that when he was in the wilderness he lived on honey and locusts. For years I imagined that he ate locust insects but in fact this refers to the locust bean. The pods are deliciously sweet and chewy and look like flattened dried bananas.

An electric mixer is always best for light wholemeal sponge mixtures but you can achieve lightness without a mixer by creaming the margarine and sugar until it is fluffy and adding the beaten eggs a spoonful at a time.

The cake is big so you will need two 10 inch (25cm) round cake tins, greased and lined, a large mixing bowl, a wooden spoon, a bowl to whisk eggs in and an egg whisk.

Imperial (Metric)	American
8 oz self-raising wholemeal flour	2 cups self-raising wholewheat flour
1 oz (25g) carob powder	¼ cup carob powder
9 oz (250g) polyunsaturated margarine	1 cup + 2 tablespoons polyunsaturated
9 oz (250g) soft dark raw cane sugar	margarine
4 large eggs	1½ cups soft dark raw cane sugar
3 drops vanilla essence	4 large eggs
	3 drops vanilla essence

1 Set the oven at 375°F/190°F (Gas Mark 5).

2 Sift flour and carob powder into a bowl.

3 In another bowl, cream the margarine and the sugar until light and fluffy (about 6 minutes).

4 Whisk the eggs together for 1 minute.

5 Add the eggs a spoonful at a time to the creamed mixture.

6 Before adding the last two or three spoonfuls, mix in a tablespoon of the flour mixture.

7 Finish adding the eggs and gradually fold in the flour and carob. Finally, add 3 drops of vanilla essence.

8 Divide the mixture equally between the prepared tins. To make sure it is equal, weigh the empty tins then weigh them again when filled.

9 Bake for 30 minutes near the centre of the oven. As you have two large tins you will not be able to put them in the centre so place one tin just above centre and one tin just below. Change them around after 15 minutes.

For the Filling and Topping:

Imperial (Metric)	American
1 carob bar	1 carob bar
¼ pint (140ml) double cream	⅔ cup heavy cream
2 tablespoons natural yogurt	2 tablespoons plain yogurt
No-added-sugar jam	No-added-sugar jam

1 Put the carob bar in a bowl. Set the bowl over a pan of boiling water and let the carob melt.

2 Whisk the cream until smooth and thick.

3 Stir in the yogurt.

4 Fold in the melted carob.

5 Put this in the fridge until cake is quite cold. The filling will set in the fridge and be easy to spread.

6 Spread a little jam (additive-free) on the top of one sponge. Spread with one-third of the filling and sandwich the other sponge onto it.

7 Now spread a thin layer of jam on top of the cake. Cover with the remainder of the filling, decorating or piping as you wish.

Orange Carob or Chocolate Buns
(Makes 18)

You will need two bun trays, 18 paper bun cases, 2 mixing bowls, a wooden spoon, another bowl for whisking eggs and a cheese grater.

Imperial (Metric)	American
5 oz (150g) self-raising wholemeal flour	1¼ cups self-raising wholewheat flour
1 oz (25g) carob or cocoa powder	¼ cup carob or cocoa powder
6 oz (175g) polyunsaturated margarine	¾ cup polyunsaturated margarine
6 oz (175g) soft dark raw cane sugar	1 cup soft dark raw cane sugar
3 large eggs	3 large eggs
Grated rind of 1 large orange	Grated rind of 1 large orange

1 Set the oven at 375°F/190°C (Gas Mark 5).

2 Sift the flour and carob or cocoa powder into a bowl.

3 In another bowl, cream the margarine and sugar until light and fluffy (about 6 minutes).

4 Beat the eggs for 1 minute.

5 Add the egg mixture, a tablespoon at a time.

6 Just before the last tablespoon is added, sprinkle 1 tablespoon of flour and carob into the mixture.

7 Gradually add the rest of the flour and carob, folding it in gently.

8 Finally add the grated orange peel.

9 Using a spoon, divide the mixture equally between the paper cases.

10 Bake one tray just above centre and one tray just below centre of the oven for 15 to 20 minutes, changing the trays around after 8 minutes.

Shortbread Triangles

These lovely biscuits melt in your mouth and are very easy to make. You will need a well-greased 9 inch (23cm) sandwich tin, a mixing bowl, a wooden spoon and cool hands to form the dough.

Imperial (Metric)	American
4 oz (100g) polyunsaturated margarine	½ cup polyunsaturated margarine
2½ oz (65g) soft dark raw cane sugar	¼ cup soft dark raw cane sugar
6 oz 100 per cent wholemeal flour	1½ cups wholewheat flour
1 tablespoon sesame seeds	1 tablespoon sesame seeds
Pinch of sea salt	Pinch of sea salt

1 Set the oven at 325°F/170°C (Gas Mark 3).

2 Cream the margarine and sugar for 3 minutes.

3 Gradually fold in the flour, sesame seeds and salt.

4 Mould the mixture well together with cool hands. Press the mixture gently but firmly into the well-greased tin.

5 Bake in the centre of the oven for 30 mins.

6 When just out of the oven cut into 16 triangles, the mixture will be soft until you let it get quite cool, so let it get cold in the tray. To keep, put in an airtight tin.

Variation:

Carob and Hazelnut Shortbread

1 Leave out the sesame seeds and add 1 tablespoon chopped hazelnuts (filberts).

2 Replace 2 level teaspoons of flour with 2 level teaspoons of carob powder.

3 To make these more delicious you could add the very finely grated rind of 1 small orange after creaming together the margarine and sugar.

Now you can see that this basic shortbread recipe could make any amount of different varieties of biscuit. You just add what you like as long as it does not change the texture.

Malted Sesame Biscuits

These are very easy to make. You will need 4 greased baking trays and a mixing bowl.

Imperial (Metric)	American
1 heaped teaspoon bicarbonate of soda (*not* baking powder)	1 heaped teaspoon baking soda (*not* baking powder)
2 teaspoons hot water	2 teaspoons hot water
4 oz (110g) polyunsaturated margarine	½ cup polyunsaturated margarine
1 generous tablespoon malt extract	1 generous tablespoon malt extract
3 oz (175g) Demerara sugar	½ cup Demerara sugar
3 oz (175g) sesame seeds	⅔ cup sesame seeds
4 oz (110g) wholemeal flour	1 cup wholewheat flour
3 oz (75g) porridge oats	¾ cup rolled oats
Pinch of sea salt	Pinch of sea salt

1 Dissolve the bicarbonate of soda (baking soda) in the hot water.

2 Melt the margarine and malt by placing a small saucepan or bowl, with the malt and margarine in it, over a pan of hot water.

3 Put all the other ingredients into a mixing bowl, then stir in the malt and margarine plus the soda and water mixture.

4 Mix all well together with your hands.

5 Form the mixture into small balls, putting 6 on each tray. (The balls spread out considerably while cooking.)

6 Cook two trays at a time placing one just above centre of the oven and one just below centre. Bake for 20 minutes, changing the tins around after 10 minutes. Cool on the tray. The biscuits harden as they cool.

Note: If the centres are not quite hard when cold just put biscuits back in the oven for 5 minutes and let them get cold again. Store in an airtight tin.

Variations:
You can make many varieties of the Malted Sesame Biscuits which taste quite different. Here is one example.

Cashew and Honey Snaps

From the Malted Sesame Biscuit recipe, take out the sesame seeds and add chopped cashew nuts. Take out the malt and add 2 level tablespoons honey. Make the recipe in exactly the same way and you will have a completely different tasting biscuit.

Popcorn Honey Crunch

There are many varieties of corn, such as sweetcorn which is eaten as corn on the cob, Dent corn and Flour corn both of which are ground into meal and cornflour. Corn meal is a wholegrain but cornflour is white and the valuable germ and fibre has been removed. Flint corn has a very hard outer layer or husk and is fed to animals, and Popcorn, which also has a hard outer layer, is of course used for making the delicious snack in this recipe.

You will need a good-sized saucepan with a *tight* lid, a mixing bowl, a fork and a baking tray, well greased. One tip: never try to pop too much corn at once. It will burn by the time the lot has popped.

Imperial (Metric)	American
5 teaspoons corn oil	5 teaspoons corn oil
3 oz (75g) popping corn	3 ounces popping corn
I tablespoon honey	I tablespoon honey
I dessertspoon malt extract	2 teaspoons malt extract
Pinch of sea salt	Pinch of sea salt

1 Set the oven at 350°F/180°C (Gas Mark 4).

2 Heat 2 teaspoons oil in a saucepan until quite hot. Add the popcorn. Wait until you hear a pop.

3 Put the lid on, turn down the heat to moderate, count to 20 and shake the pan, still with the lid on. Do this several times until the popping stops. Shaking makes the unpopped corn fall to the bottom to be popped.

4 Place the popped corn into a bowl.

5 Melt the honey, malt, oil and a pinch of salt on a low heat. Do not overheat.

6 Stir this into the corn, mixing well together.

7 Spread the mixture onto a greased baking tray.

8 Bake for 10 to 15 minutes until golden-brown. Take care not to burn.

9 Wait until the corn is quite cold. It will then become crunchy. If it is not all eaten (which of course it will be!) store in an airtight container.

Fruit and Nut Slice

This last tea-time recipe is a great in-between mealtime filler. Highly nutritious and great for keeping off those bars of chocolate. It's very simple to make but you will need a mincer. You will also need a bowl. You can make the mixture into several shapes, which I will describe below.

Imperial (Metric)	American
6 oz (175g) stoned dates	I cup pitted dates
3 oz (75g) dried apricots	I cup dried apricots
6 oz (175g) raisins	I cup raisins
6 oz (175g) mixed nuts and sunflower seeds	I ¼ cups mixed nuts and sunflower seeds
A few sesame seeds for coating	A few sesame seeds for coating

1 Wash the apricots well and pat dry in kitchen paper.

2 Mix the dried fruit with the nuts and sunflower seeds and gradually put them through the mincer.

3 When it is all minced, press the mixture well together, kneading for 1 minute at least.

4 Either form into a long thin loaf shape for slicing later or make rectangular bars approximately 3 inches (7.5cm) long and 1½ inches (3.5cm) wide. Coat in sesame seeds and press the seeds gently in.

5 Alternatively, roll the mixture into a long sausage shape. Roll the sausage in sesame seeds pressing them gently but firmly in. Slice in little circles. To keep, put in an airtight tin. They will last several weeks.

Herbal Teas and Other Healthy Beverages

We are all familiar with the traditional cups of tea, coffee and cocoa, but these drinks contain large amounts of caffeine and tannin, both of which can be harmful to your health if taken too frequently.

I would like to introduce you to a few tasty beverages that positively benefit your health.

Drinking a herb tea means that you are absorbing the goodness of health-giving plants and being refreshed at the same time. There are hundreds of different varieties but I will give you just a few popular teas to start you off.

You can buy herb tea bags but it's much more interesting to buy the herbs loose and experiment with different combinations to suit your own taste.

Rose Hip and Hibiscus

Both contain generous amounts of vitamin C. The tea made from these is a deep rich red and has a citrus taste. Delicious hot or cold. To make 3 cups bring water to the boil and heat the teapot with a little hot water. Rinse. Add 1 rounded teaspoon Rose Hip powder and 1 rounded teaspoon ground Hibiscus to the pot. Pour on 3 cups of boiling water. Cover and leave to stand for 5 minutes. Serve with a little honey to sweeten.

Peppermint and Hibiscus

This is a delightful tea hot or cold. To make three cups, simply bring water to boil, heat the teapot, rinse and add 1 rounded teaspoon Peppermint and 1 rounded teaspoon ground Hibiscus to the pot. Pour three cups of boiling water over this and cover. Leave to stand for 5 minutes.

Lemon Verbena

The tea made from this is very delicate. To make three cups, boil the water, heat the teapot, rinse, add two teaspoons of the leaves and three cups of boiling water. Leave to stand covered for *2 minutes only*. The tea is then at its best. Standing any longer makes the tea bitter.

Basil and Orange

Many of you will, no doubt, have used basil when cooking but this herb makes a lovely tea when mixed with orange peel. To make three cups bring water to boil, heat the pot, rinse, put in two teaspoons basil and a complete curl of thin orange peel (make sure there is no white pith on the peel). Cover and leave to stand for 5 minutes.

Camomile

Good for calming the nerves. Great for babies when teething and wakeful, but only give them half a cup. To make three cups bring water to boil, heat the pot, rinse and add two teaspoons camomile flowers plus three cups boiling water. Leave to stand, covered, for 5 to 7 minutes. Serve with a very little honey if you wish, especially if giving this to a baby.

Barley Cup or Grain Coffee

There are many different varieties of grain coffee on the market. The cheapest is Barley Cup and I think this is the one to try if you want a satisfying drink instead of regular coffee or cocoa. All you do is add 1 good teaspoon per cup, pour boiling water over this and add a little milk. Or you can make this with half milk and half water if you like. It's certainly worth a try.

Carob Drink — Hot or Ice-creamed

Delicious hot or ice cold in summer with a dollop of ice-cream for an extra treat.

Imperial (Metric)	American
1 pint (570ml) milk	2½ cups milk
2 rounded teaspoons carob powder	2 rounded teaspoons carob powder
1 vanilla pod (*or* 2 drops vanilla essence)	1 vanilla pod (*or* 2 drops vanilla essence)
¼ teaspoon cinnamon powder (optional)	¼ teaspoon cinnamon powder (optional)
2 teaspoons honey *or* Barbados sugar, to taste	2 teaspoons honey *or* Barbados sugar, to taste

1 Whisk all ingredients together in a bowl. Pour into a saucepan and bring gently to boil. Let it simmer very gently for 1 minute only.

2 Drink hot or pour into a jug and let it get quite cold in the fridge. When serving cold, strain the skin off. Stir, pour into glasses and as a special treat put a dollop of ice-cream into each glass. Pop a straw in and enjoy it.

Carob Banana Cooler

If you have a liquidizer you could liquidize the cold carob drink above with 2 bananas until smooth and then add the ice-cream. This is extra delicious!

INDEX